how to make
paper planes
and other flying objects

how to make
paper planes
and other flying objects

35 STEP-BY-STEP OBJECTS TO FLY IN AN INSTANT

MARI ONO AND
ROSHIN ONO

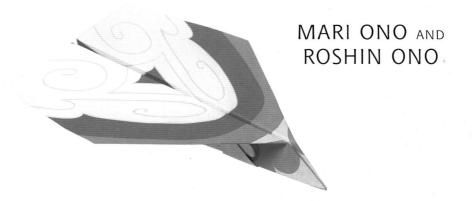

CICO BOOKS

LONDON NEW YORK

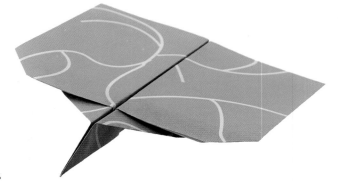

For my father and Roshin's granddad,
Eiji Tamaki

Editor: Robin Gurdon
Designer: Paul Tilby
Photography: Geoff Dann
Photograghy styling and
illustration: Trina Dalziel

First published in 2010 by CICO Books under
ISBN 978 1 907030 59 8

This edition published in 2012 by CICO Books
An imprint of Ryland Peters & Small
20–21 Jockey's Fields
London WC1R 4BW

519 Broadway, 5th Floor
New York, NY 10012

10 9 8 7 6 5 4 3 2 1

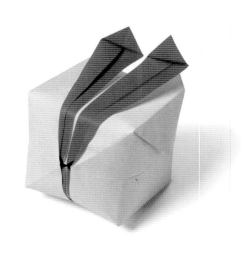

A CIP catalog record for this book is
available from the Library of Congress
and the British Library.

ISBN 978 1 908862 53 2

Printed in China

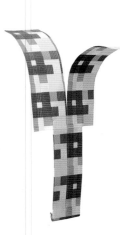

Contents

INTRODUCTION

The ancient art of *origami*—the creation of models from a single sheet of folded paper—has been part of Japanese culture for many centuries. In its homeland, *origami* has a special place, being on one hand the happy pastime of children while also being an important symbol of the culture of traditional manners, similar in its own way to the tea ceremony and the art of flower arranging. *Origami* is now becoming more well-known around the world, gaining popularity with many adults in the same way as with children.

This book introduces many of the flying model planes that have become especially popular. *How to Make Paper Planes and Other Flying Objects* contains many that have been designed specifically for this book though, of course, they all retain a hint of the traditional *origami* planes of Japan. The making of paper planes has developed from a schoolroom pastime into a serious, competitive pursuit whose aim is to see which models can fly farthest and longest—it is now so popular that the records are even included in the *Guinness Book of Records*!

However, with this book we hope to encourage you to play not just with paper planes but we are also introducing designs for animals, birds, and insects that fly and float, as well as *origami* kites that everyone can easily make and a selection of *origami* toys that can be happily thrown and bounced about.

We also hope that this book will inspire you to create new paper planes and kites of your original design based, perhaps, on your favorite jet or the passenger plane that took you on vacation. Kites can be variously transformed by amending the design or simply changing their size or the materials of the tail.

Making a paper plane or a kite with friends, parents, or grandparents can also be a happy way of getting together. *Origami* is wonderful way of playing as it doesn't need any advanced techniques and can be enjoyed by every age group. In addition, there is little as energizing as the achievement of completing a difficult *origami* model—the end product will give you a great sense of accomplishment.

So now let your creativity loose on the wings of your paper planes and fly away into the sky with the models on the following pages!

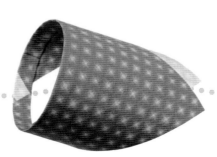

BASIC TECHNIQUES

Origami is a very simple craft that anyone from the smallest child upward can master. All that is required is a steady hand and some patience. Before you start making your first plane just check over these simple tips to ensure every paper model you make is a success.

MAKING FOLDS

Making the paper fold as crisply and evenly as possible is the key to making models that will fly as the designs intend—it really is as simple as that.

1 When you make a fold ensure that the paper lies exactly where you want it, with the corners sitting exactly on top of each other.

2 As you make the crease ensure you keep the paper completely still so that the fold is perfectly true and straight.

3 Still holding the paper with your spare hand use a ruler or perhaps the side of a pencil to press down the fold until it is as flat as possible.

OPENING FOLDS

Sometimes you will need to open out a crease and refold the paper so that it lies in a new shape, as in the triangle fold shown here.

1 Lift the flap to be opened out and begin pulling the two sides apart.

2 As the space widens you will need to ensure that the far point folds true, so use a pencil to gently prise the paper open.

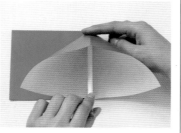

3 As the two corners separate the top point drops forward and the two edges open out to become one.

4 Press down the new creases to make the two new angled sides of the triangle.

REVERSING FOLDS

To reverse a crease, as on the nose of the plane here, you will need to open out your model and gently turn part of the paper back on itself. This can sometimes be tricky so practice on an old model first.

1 To turn the nose back on itself first make a firm crease with a simple fold.

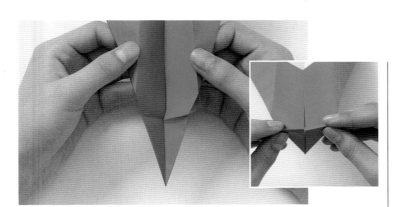

2 Let the nose back and open out the model then turn back the nose again along the fold you just made.

3 When you close the model together again the nose has reversed and is now flat.

KEY TO ARROWS

FOLD
Fold the part of the paper shown in this direction.

FOLDING DIRECTION
Fold the entire paper over in this direction.

OPEN OUT
Open out and refold the paper over in the direction shown.

CHANGE THE POSITION
Spin the paper 90° in the direction of the arrows.

CHANGE THE POSITION
Spin the paper through 180°.

TURN OVER
Turn the paper over.

MAKE A CREASE
Fold the paper over in the direction of the arrow then open it out again.

FLYING SCHOOL

All of the planes and kites as well as many of the animals and toys will fly, though there are many different ways to launch them. Follow the instructions below and then practice to find the best way to achieve a long flight.

PLANES

Many of the planes are folded so that they have central bodies. Always check your creases are sharp and the paper is smooth before you throw it. Grip the plane between your thumb and forefinger to launch.

CLASSIC PLANE—PAGE 18

ROSS-17—PAGE 48

VERTICAL TAIL—PAGE 42

SUNLIGHT—PAGE 36

INTO THE AIR

To achieve really long flights it can be helpful to throw the model high into the air. Use as much power as you can and practice to find the angle that works best. Experiment by making small adjustments to the angle of the wings to help the plane fly straighter or higher.

1 Start by holding the plane low next to your ankles with your knees bent.

2 As you raise the plane lift your body as well.

3 Point the plane high into the sky and swivel your body to gain as much power as possible when you let go.

THROWING WINGS

Some of the planes do not have bodies to grasp so they are more difficult to launch a significant distance. All of them will fly with a flick of the wrist.

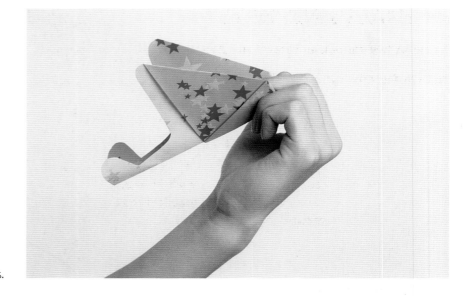

1 Grip the front of the plane from underneath with the tips of your fingers.

2 Flick your hand forward from the wrist to launch.

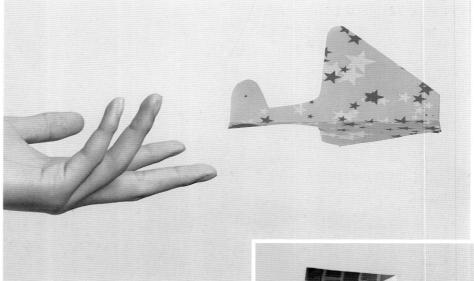

3 Ensure your fingers end up pointing in the direction you want the plane to fly. The flying brick (see page 40) should also be launched in this way.

ANIMALS AND TOYS

Some of the animals and toys will also fly
but each has its own special way of flying.

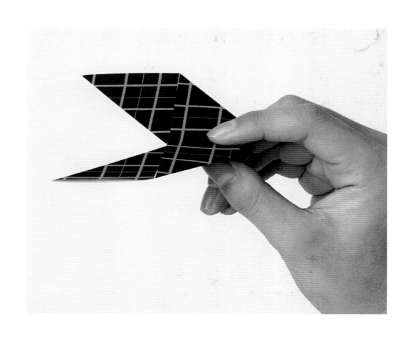

CICADA—PAGE 80

The cicada is an insect that appears to flit
across the sky. Hold the model between
your thumb and forefinger and flick it
forward to see it spin across the room.

MAGIC RING—PAGE 110

The magic ring looks like it shouldn't fly.
Hold it with your fingers and throw it
forward to see it fly as far as any plane!

KITES—PAGES 64–77

All the kites in this book will fly
in a gentle breeze. Take the kite
outside, run into a breeze, and
unwind the thread attached to
its body, little by little. The wind
should lift it up into the sky.

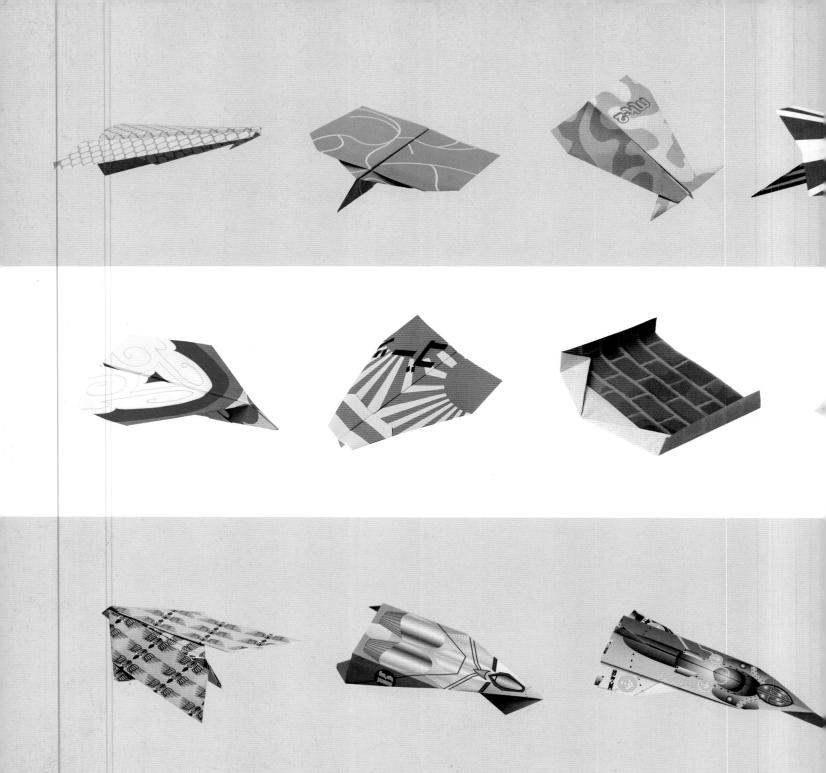

PLANES *aplenty*

01 CLASSIC PLANE

Although the exact origins of *origami* have never been discovered it has been one of the most popular forms of play for Japanese children for centuries. For many years the secrets of the art have been handed down from one generation to another, ensuring that the designs flourished. This classic paper airplane is a model that has been much loved for generations because it flies very well even though it is so quick and easy to fold.

You will need
1 sheet of 6in (15cm) square paper

1 Make a crease down the center of the paper by folding it in half then opening it out again. Turn in the corners of one end of the paper so that the sides lie along the central crease with the corners next to each other.

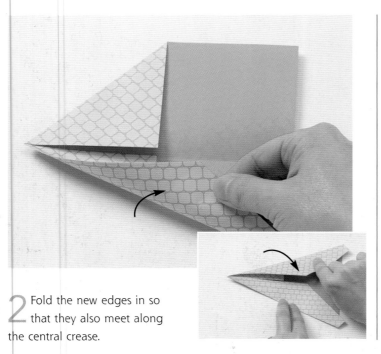

2 Fold the new edges in so that they also meet along the central crease.

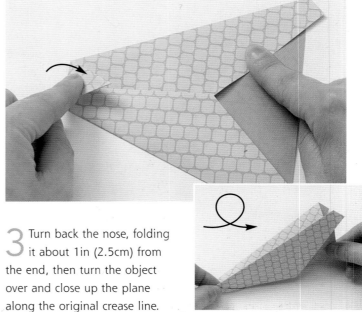

3 Turn back the nose, folding it about 1in (2.5cm) from the end, then turn the object over and close up the plane along the original crease line.

PLANES APLENTY

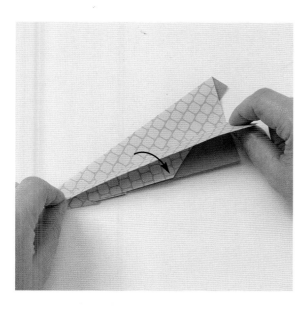

4 Turn over the wing at a slight angle so that the
plane's body is deeper at the back than the front.

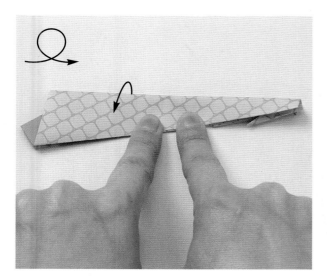

5 Turn the plane over and fold down the other wing so
that it exactly matches the first then open out the
wings so that they sit together, at right angles to the body.

02 GLIDER

This simple glider is a cinch to make and is a brilliant flyer. With a gentle throw it will glide far and long, putting some of the more technical planes to shame. The trick is the double fold on the nose; it adds a bit of weight and helps it to go that extra bit farther.

You will need
1 sheet of 6in (15cm) square paper
Paper glue

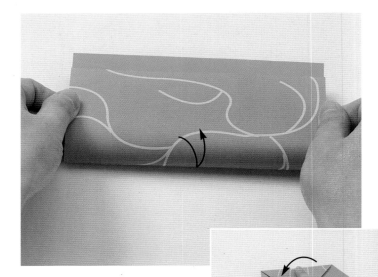

1 Fold the paper in half and open it out to make a crease then turn in the corners at one end so that they meet along the center crease.

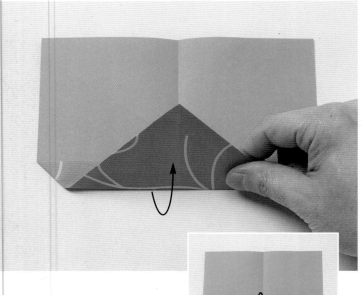

2 Fold back the nose, making the crease about 1¼in (3cm) inside the folds made in the previous step then fold it back on itself, making the crease about ⅝in (1.5cm) from the first fold.

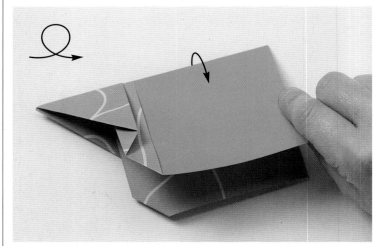

3 Turn the whole paper over and fold the object in half along the central crease.

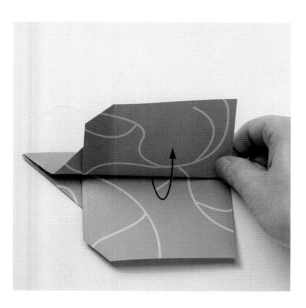

4 Turn back the top wing making the fold parallel to, and approximately 1¼in (3cm) up from, the bottom of the plane. Turn the model over and repeat on the other side.

5 Add a dab of glue inside the body of the plane and press together to ensure the two wings sit together.

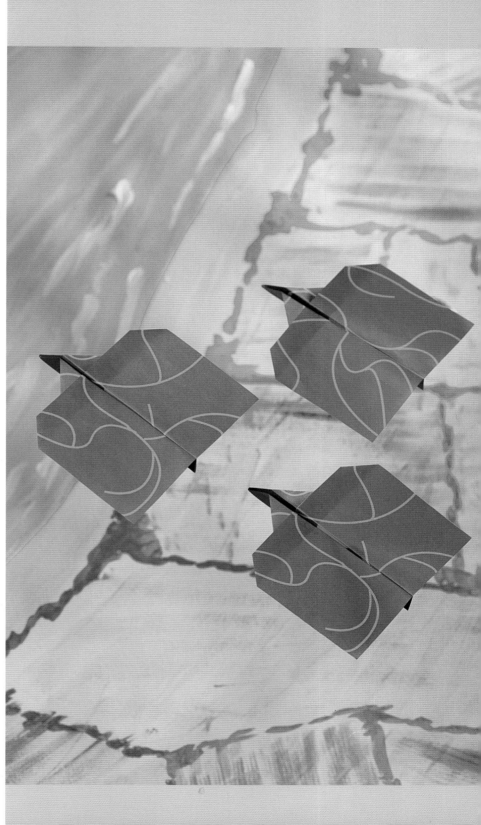

03 STEALTH JET

This jet is a classic in Japan and has been made by paper plane enthusiasts for generations. It is known as the "Squid Airplane" in Japan because its shape looks like a sea squid! Try applying some glue to the center of the plane—this will hold it together and help it to fly better.

Skill rating ● ● ○

You will need
1 sheet of A5 (8¼x6in/21x15cm) paper
Paper glue

1 Make a crease along the center of the paper by folding the colored sides together. Open out the sheet and fold two corners to meet along the central crease.

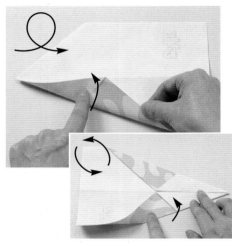

2 Turn the paper over and fold both angled edges in to meet along the central crease.

3 Lift up the object and open out the two loose flaps of paper at the pointed end.

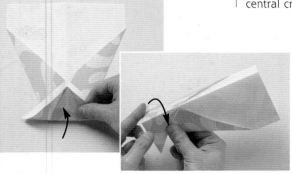

4 Turn back the pointed end making the fold between the two outer points then lift the object and fold it in half along the central crease.

5 Lift the top flap forward to make the wing, making a straight fold about ½in (1.5cm) up from the bottom. Turn the paper over and repeat, then place a little paper glue in the space between the wings and press together.

04 THUNDERSTORM

The Thunderstorm is an exciting plane that will slice quickly through the air. With its large wing span it will fly far and true if you throw it with a bit of power up toward the sky. When you make this model plane take care to turn over the nose just enough so that the wings sit together without the need for any glue.

Skill rating ● ● ○

You will need
1 sheet of A5 (8¼x6in/21x15cm) paper

1 Fold the paper in half to make a crease then open it out again. Fold in the corners at one end to meet along the center line and then repeat, folding the angled sides so that they meet in the middle.

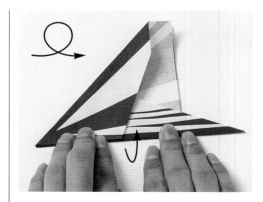

2 Fold back the end of the plane, making a crease about 5in (12.5cm) from the rear of the object.

3 Turn the paper over and fold the back edges of the plane forward, angled so that they meet along the center line.

4 Turn the object over and fold it in half along the central crease.

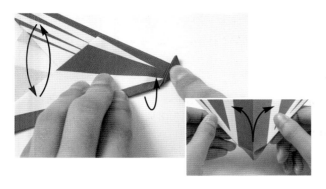

5 Spin the object round and fold the tip of the nose across the main crease line then open out the paper.

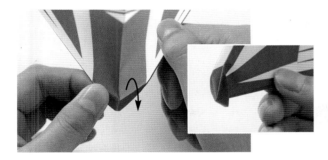

6 Gently reverse the creases made when you turned over the nose and push the object back together so that the nose now points downward.

7 Fold the wings down, making the creases parallel to the bottom of the plane and starting just behind the turned nose.

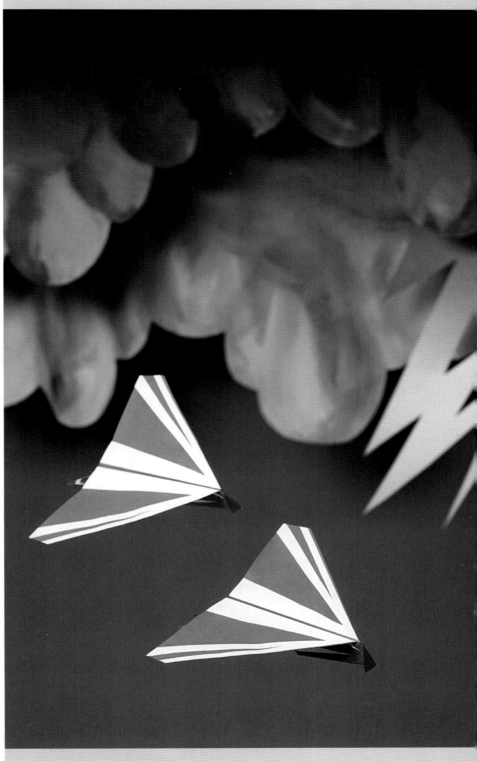

05 STAR STRIKE

The Star Strike is an airplane that is designed to fly fast and far, resembling a comet hurtling through outer space. Try playing with the Star Strike indoors in a large room—perhaps the gym at school—throwing it high into the air toward the ceiling where it can fly before gliding gracefully back down to earth.

You will need
1 sheet of A5 (8¼x6in/21x15cm) paper

1 Fold the paper in half lengthways and open out to leave a crease, then fold in the corners at one end to meet along the center line.

2 Fold in the angled edges so that they also meet along the central crease line.

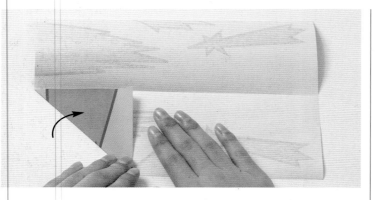

3 Spin the paper round and fold back the tip, making a crease about 3in (7.5cm) in, ensuring that the tip just covers the point where the diagonal edges meet in the center of the paper.

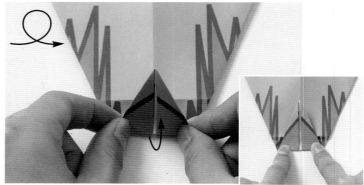

4 Turn the paper over and open out the nose before folding it back on itself, making a crease approximately 2in (5cm) from the end.

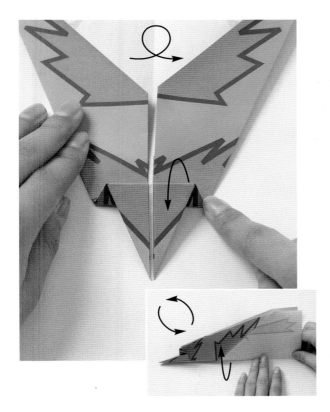

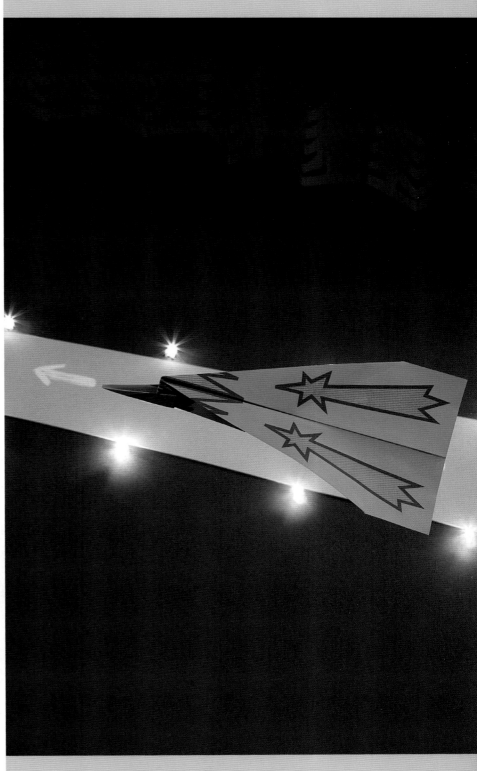

5 Turn the paper back over and fold up the nose using the two creases just made, then spin the object and fold it together along the central crease.

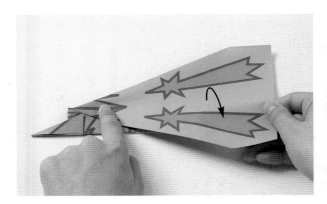

6 Fold down the wings with creases parallel to the base of the plane at the closest possible point to the nose.

06 STAR LIGHT

The Star Light is a traditional paper plane model in Japan. There it is called the "Swallow Plane" as it closely resembles the bird's swooping shape and flies with the same easy style as well. It does not have a body like most paper planes and flies in a unique way as it is thrown by a flick of your fingers out of the back of your hand. Although this method looks a little awkward at first, with practice the Star Light will fly as well as any plane.

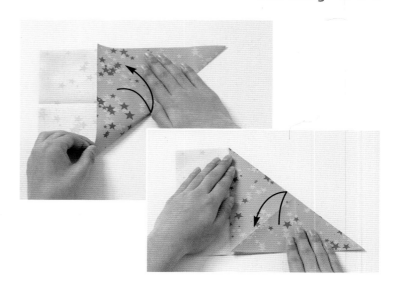

You will need
1 sheet of A5 (8¼x6in/21x15cm) paper
Scissors

1 First, fold the paper in half lengthwise and open out to make a crease. Next fold the corners of one end across to the other side of the paper opening both out to make diagonal creases.

2 Fold the right-hand end of the paper over, using the crossing point of the diagonal creases as the marker for the fold.

3 Fold the corners into the center using the diagonal creases made earlier as the fold lines.

4 Open out the last folds and lift the nearest corner, taking it across to the other side of the paper so that the flap opens out before refolding it to form a triangle.

5 Fold the far point of the triangle back over to the near side of the object.

6 Lift the far point, opening out the flap and folding it toward you, forming another triangle.

7 Fold the top flap back over so that there is one flap on each side of the object.

9 Fold the sides of the central diamond across the center so that they meet along the center line.

8 Fold the corners of both top flaps over so that the corners meet at the object's end point.

10 Lift the paper and use scissors to cut along the center line from the tip to the point at which the two folds made in the last step meet.

11 Lift the top flaps and gently open them out with a finger or a pencil then turn back each side of the nose and tuck them into the holes until the crease is flush.

12 Turn the object over and fold it in half along the central crease.

13 Use the scissors to cut out the shape of the wings and tail.

07 BLUE BIRD

The blue bird is very cool! Throw it gently without using much force, letting the bird catch the breeze with its long, sleek shape. Get together with your friends and make enough blue birds to create a flock.

Skill rating ● ● ○

You will need
1 sheet of A5 (8¼x6in/21x15cm) paper

1 Fold the paper in half lengthwise before opening out to leave a crease. Next fold in the corners at one end so that they meet along the central crease.

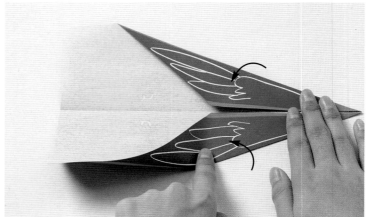

2 Fold in the angled edges so that they also meet along the center crease line.

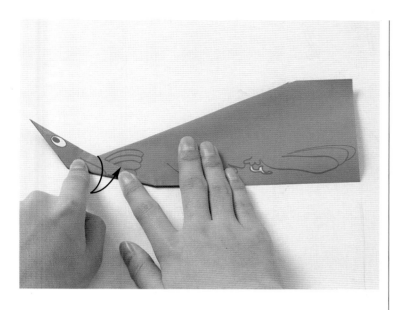

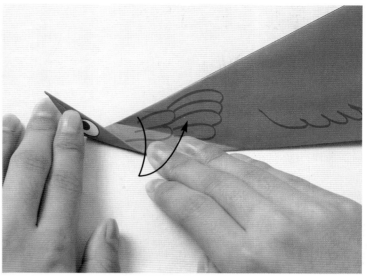

3 Fold the object in half then turn the nose upward at a shallow angle about 7.5cm (3in) from the tip to make a crease.

4 Open out the nose then fold it up again at the same angle as before but this time about 5cm (2in) from the tip.

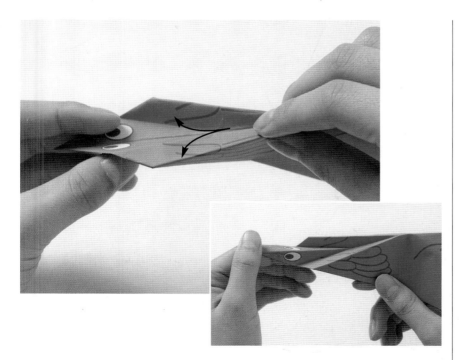

5 Open out the nose then press down between the two digaonal folds to reverse the crease and refold it.

6 Fold down the wings so that the creases are parallel to the base of the object.

08 SCATTERED CLOUDS

Skill rating ● ● ○

The Scattered Clouds plane is a record breaker when it comes to flying long distances. To achieve the best results it is especially important to be accurate with the folds and make sure that every crease has been firmly pressed in place with a ruler. To fly high toward the sky, boost the length of your flight with a jump as you release the airplane into the air.

You will need
1 sheet of A5 (8¼x6in/21x15cm) paper

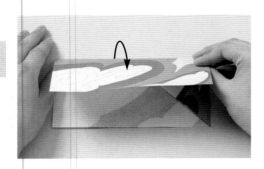

1 Make a crease along the center of the paper then open out and fold the corners at one end into the middle. Next fold over the pointed end using the edges of the previous folds as guides.

2 Fold the top half of the paper forward along the central crease.

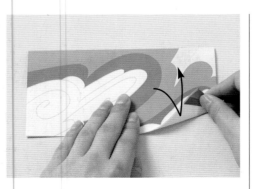

3 Turn up the bottom corner at a slight angle and make a crease.

4 Open out the paper and fold in the two corners along the creases made in the previous step.

Fold in the flaps so that the bottom edges meet along the central crease.

34

PLANES APLENTY

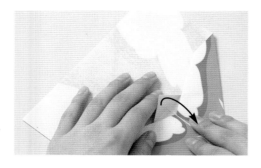

6 Fold forward the small triangle of paper sticking out from under the flaps so that it covers the flaps made in the previous step.

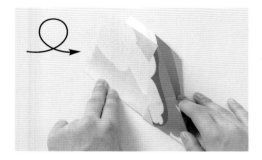

7 Turn the paper over and fold it together along the central crease, ensuring that the small triangle from the last step is still pointing forward.

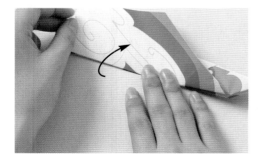

8 Turn over the wings with creases parallel to the base of the model to finish.

09 SUNLIGHT

The Sunlight is one of the fastest and most stable airplane designs. Its wide wing cuts through the wind, allowing it to fly straight and true, covering a good distance. Extend the duration of the flight even further by throwing it high up into the air. Although the paper used here is A5 (8¼x6in/21x15cm), you can use a larger sheet of rectangular paper to make a bigger plane—which should also fly farther.

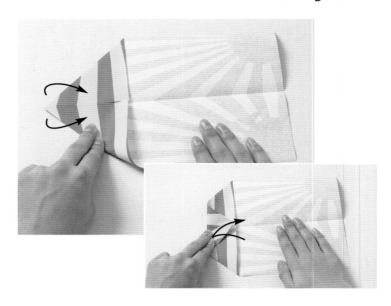

You will need
1 sheet of A5 (8¼x6in/21x15cm) paper

1 Fold lengthwise to make a crease then open out and fold the corners at one end into the center. Now fold the tip back so that the point lies at the point where the corners meet and make a crease.

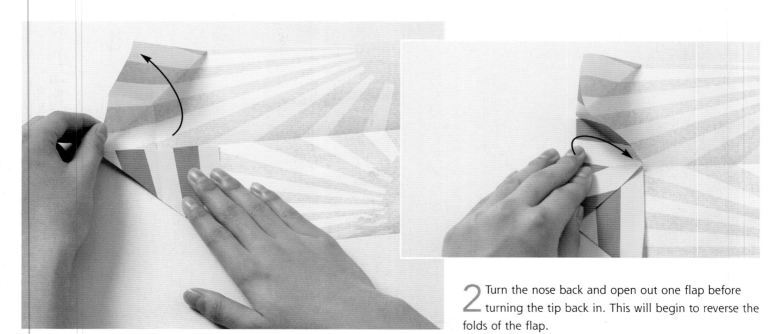

2 Turn the nose back and open out one flap before turning the tip back in. This will begin to reverse the folds of the flap.

3 Reverse the diagonal crease against the main sheet of paper and bring the corner to lie on the central crease.

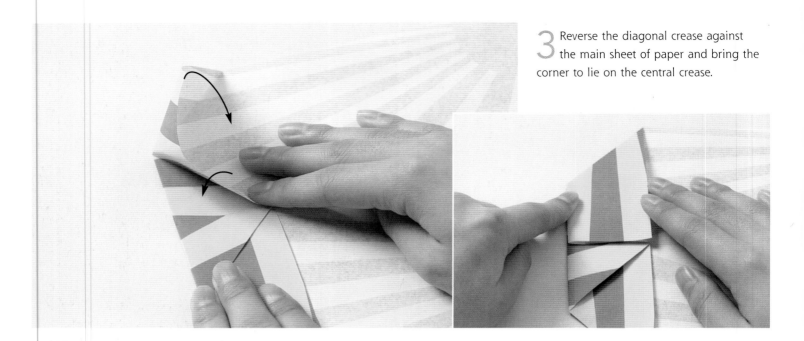

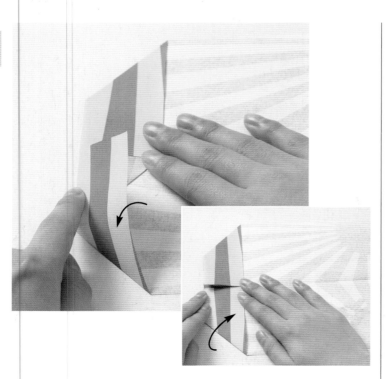

4 Open out the flap again to lift the nearer corner up then repeat the reversal of the creases and flatten.

5 Turn the whole paper over and fold the end back on itself.

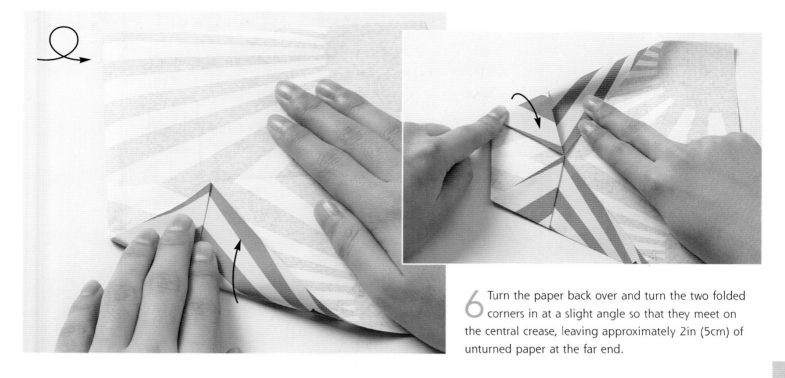

6 Turn the paper back over and turn the two folded corners in at a slight angle so that they meet on the central crease, leaving approximately 2in (5cm) of unturned paper at the far end.

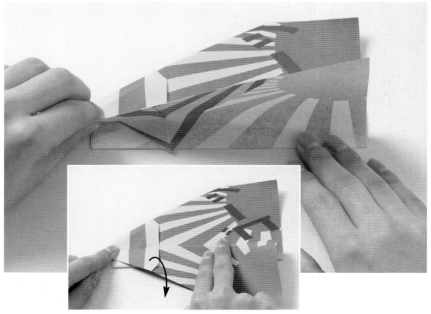

7 Lift the paper up and fold the nearer half behind.

8 Fold down the wings, making the crease parallel with the base of the plane about halfway up the flat nose.

10 BRICK

Make your friends laugh with this comedy airplane—they definitely will have never seen a brick glide effortlessly through the sky before! At first glance the brick shouldn't stay in the air because of its weight and clumsy appearance but in fact it defies all logic and flies really well.

Skill rating ● ○ ○

You will need
1 sheet of A5 (8¼×6in/21x15cm) paper

1 With the printed side up, fold the paper in half widthwise to make a crease and open out. Next fold one end into the center and then fold the same side in half again.

2 Fold the paper in half crossways but do not make a crease. Just press down the near point to mark the center and open out.

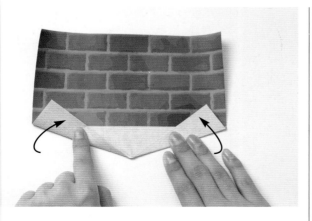

3 Turn over the folded corners, using the center mark made in the previous step as the fold point, ensuring that the sides match.

4 Turn up the wing tips using the folded corners as the marker points.

11 VERTICAL TAIL

The Vertical Tail is a classic paper airplane which you can fine-tune to improve its performance. Discover the best design by experimenting with different tail fin sizes, then testing each one to find the one which flies farthest. You will immediately see the difference your adjustments can make to the paper plane's stability, so just choose your favorite. The design on the paper is inspired by the model's flying ability and is based on the idea of an airplane that can travel high into the atmosphere.

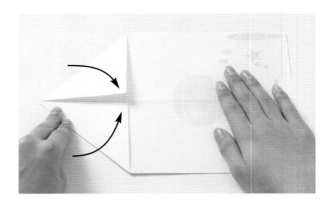

1 Make a crease down the middle of the paper then open it out and fold the corners at one end into the center.

PLANES APLENTY

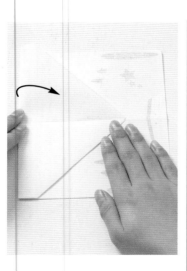

2 Turn over the nose and fold, ensuring the fold is at right angles by placing the tip along the central crease. Make the fold line about 1in (2.5cm) nearer the middle than the edge of the folds.

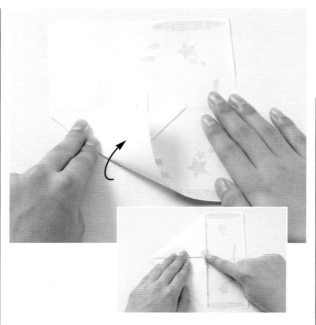

3 Fold the corners into the center then fold the small triangle that remains visible back over to hold the folds in place.

4 Lift the paper up and fold the nearer half behind along the central crease.

5 Turn over the far end of the central crease at an angle then open out the plane and reverse the creases before closing up the plane once more.

6 Turn down the wing leaving the body of the plane with a depth of no more than 3/8in (1cm) and repeat on the other side.

12 SPARROW

The sparrow is a very popular wild bird that lives all across Japan. This model is designed to resemble the bird's appearance as it quickly darts through the sky with its small body and large angled wings. The best way to ensure a successful flight is to hold the front part of the airplane between your fingertips and to launch it with a flick of the wrist.

You will need
1 sheet of 6in (15cm) square paper

PLANES APLENTY

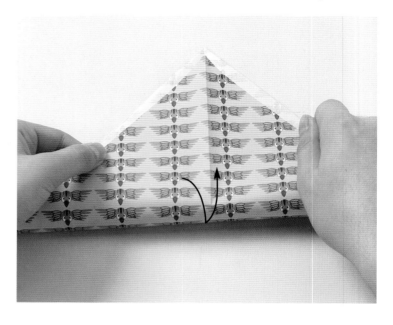

1 Fold the paper in half from corner to corner then open out and repeat in the other direction.

2 Fold one corner toward its opposite, making a crease about 1½in (4cm) from the central crease, then lift up the paper and fold the near half of the paper back underneath along the central crease.

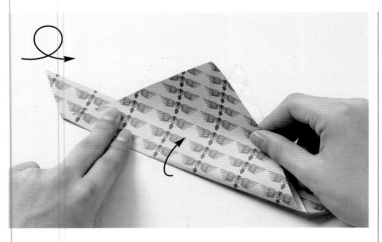

3 Turn the paper over then fold the nearest point back over the previous fold so that it lies on top of the opposite point.

4 Fold the left-hand arm up and over at an angle, using the central crease as the fold point and ensuring that the top left point finishes higher than the top center point of the object.

5 Fold the left-hand side of the paper over using the central crease as the fold line.

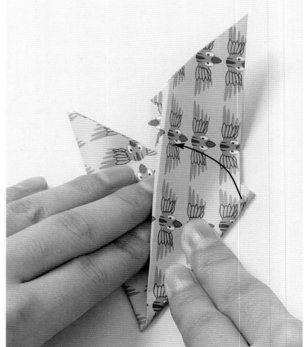

6 Turn over the right-hand arm so that it sits exactly on top of the other one.

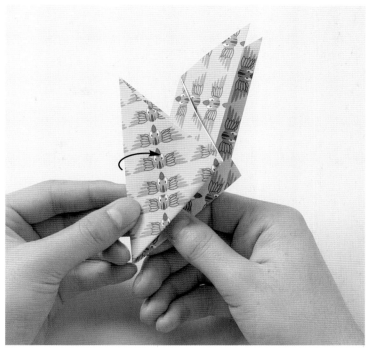

7 Open out the object by unfolding the right-hand arm then refold it so that it sits opposite the other arm.

8 Close up the paper by folding it in half along the central crease.

9 Fold back the wing with a new angled crease which also gives the Sparrow a small nose, then turn the object over and repeat on the other side.

10 Finally open out the plane and make its wings even.

13 ROSS-17

The Ross-17 is taking flight into a new age with a design that will see airplanes going deeper into outer space than ever before. This model flies best when the creases are thin and the folds sharp, which will stop the paper around the cockpit from becoming too thick and unwieldy. Take your time, though, as the folds you need to make this plane can be a little complex.

You will need
1 sheet of A5 (8¼x6in/21x15cm) paper

1 First, fold the paper along its length to make a crease and open out. Next fold one corner right across to the other side of the paper to make a diagonal crease and open out before repeating on the other side.

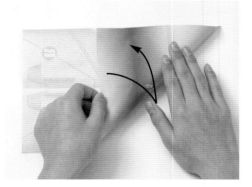

PLANES APLENTY

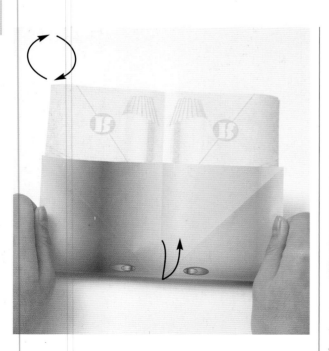

2 Turn over the end of the paper and make a fold where the diagonal creases cross.

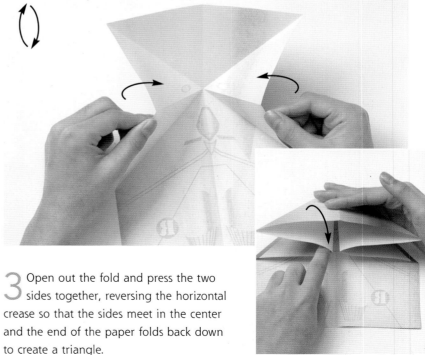

3 Open out the fold and press the two sides together, reversing the horizontal crease so that the sides meet in the center and the end of the paper folds back down to create a triangle.

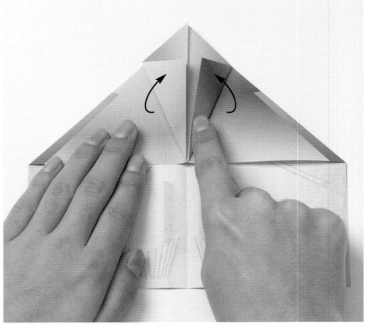

4 Fold back the top flap on each side so that the tips meet at the top of the paper and the edges lie up the central crease.

5 Fold in the sides of the diamond so that the edges meet along the middle with the flat edges of the triangles facing forward.

6 Turn back the top layers of the end point and tuck them into the flaps made in the previous step.

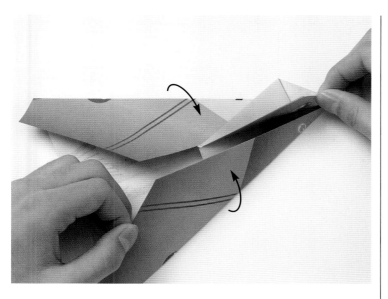

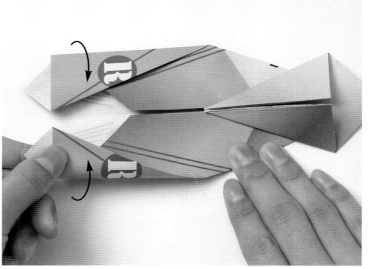

7 Lift up the sides of the diamond and fold the wing in underneath then let the diamond fall back into place.

8 Turn over the wing tips so that the points lie about 1cm (3/8in) apart directly along the bottom edge of the paper.

9 Form the wing tips into shape and press up the sides of the diamond so they are angled symmetrically to the plane.

10 Place your first finger between the sides of the diamond to keep the flaps in shape when you throw the paper plane.

14 X-12

The X-12 has been designed to resemble one of the modern jet fighters seen in popular Japanese cartoons. Its sleek shape and polished look make it perfect for aerial assaults in the backyard. And make sure you get those creases nice and straight by using a ruler. When you are flying your plane with friends take care not to throw it straight toward them because the point is a bit sharp and a direct hit could hurt them!

You will need
1 sheet of A5 (8¼x6in/21x15cm) paper

PLANES APLENTY

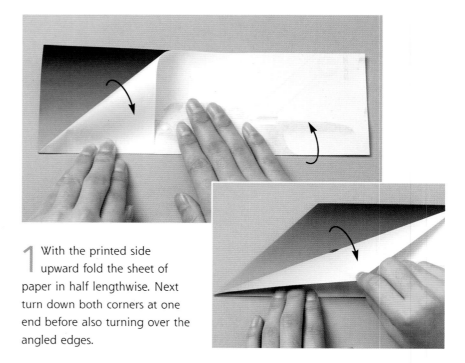

1 With the printed side upward fold the sheet of paper in half lengthwise. Next turn down both corners at one end before also turning over the angled edges.

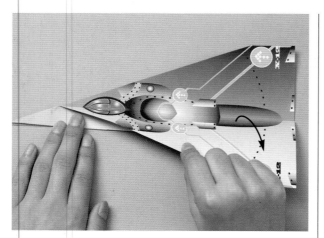

2 Turn over the wing, making the fold along the line of the cockpit so that the designs on both sides of the plane match.

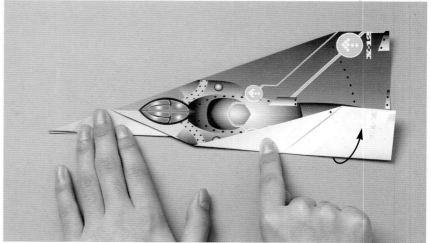

3 Fold back the outer half of the wing, starting the fold line at the edge of the design at the front.

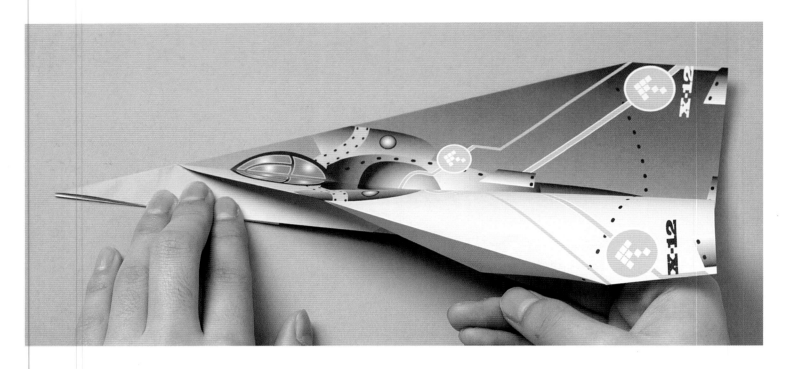

4 Reopen the flap and lift the entire wing, opening out the flap underneath with your fingers.

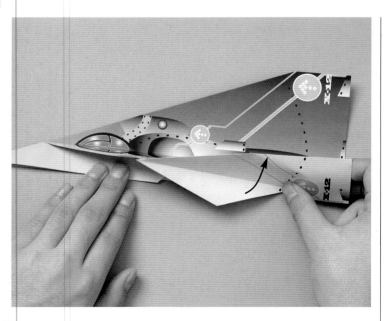

5 Reclose the wing, reversing the diagonal crease.

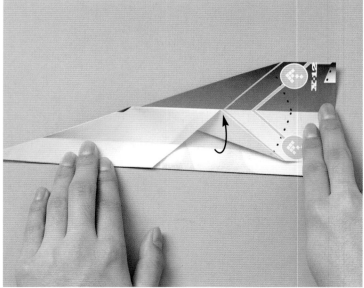

6 Press the wing flat against the other side of the plane and check the folds match the photograph.

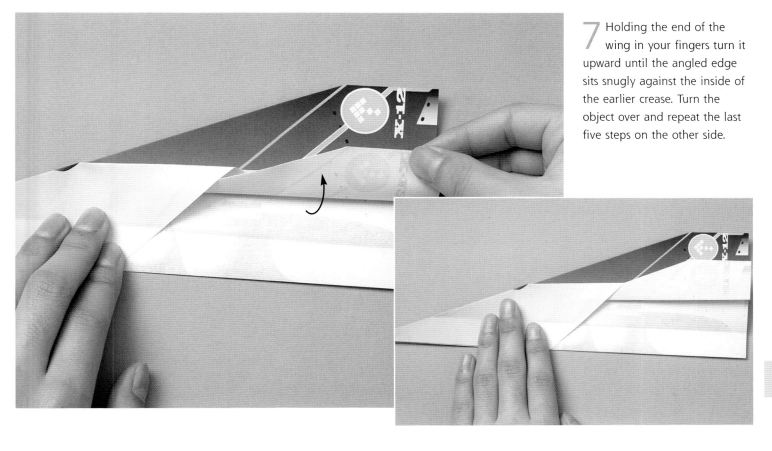

7 Holding the end of the wing in your fingers turn it upward until the angled edge sits snugly against the inside of the earlier crease. Turn the object over and repeat the last five steps on the other side.

8 Make a long, shallow angled flap at the base of the back of the plane.

9 Open out the plane and reverse the crease from the previous step so that it sticks out above the plane as a tail fin.

15 FLYING FISH

The flying fish skims over the surface of the sea, leaping over the waves, almost like an airplane flying over water. By swimming with great power it can break through the water into the air, using its momentum to make a seemingly unending series of jumps. And the sleek lines of this plane successfully replicate the grace and agility of the fish.

You will need
1 sheet of A5 (8¼x6in/21x15cm) paper
Paper glue

1 Make a crease along the middle of the paper then it open out and fold the corners at one end into the center.

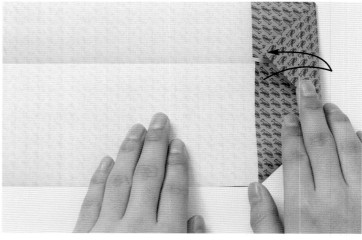

2 Now fold the tip back so that the point lies on top of the folded corners and make a crease.

3 Turn the nose back and open out one flap before turning the tip of the object back in. This will begin to reverse the folds of the flap.

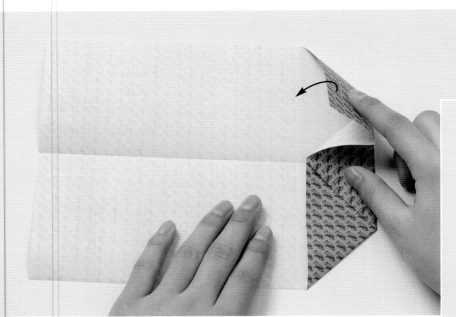

4 Reverse the diagonal crease against the main sheet of paper and bring the point down so that it lies on the central crease.

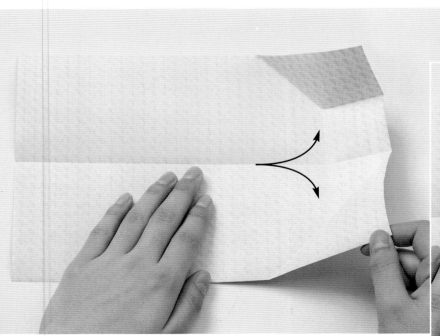

5 Open out the entire sheet. Reverse the creases on the other side and fold both sides back in together.

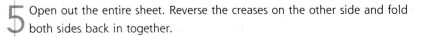

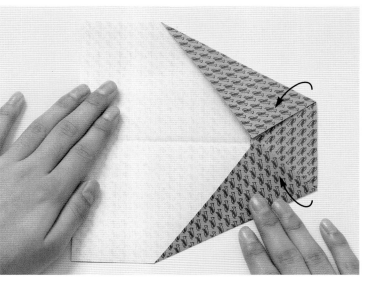

6 Turn over the folded end of the paper, making a crease along the edge of the previous folds.

7 Fold both corners in so that they meet in the middle of the edge folded in the previous step.

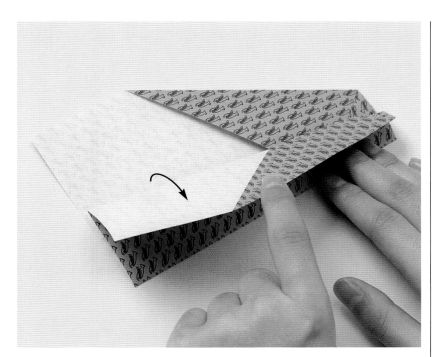

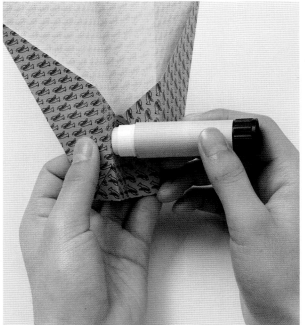

8 Close up the paper along the central crease and turn down the wings.

9 To keep the plane's shape dab some paper glue along the inside of the body and press together.

16 ROARING FIRE

This airplane will light up the sky with its roaring fire. The flames will seem to glide behind the model as they flare across its wings. The large wing area, made by first folding the paper across its width, helps this airplane stay aloft. A powerful launch lifting it high into the air will see it blaze a trail across the sky.

You will need
1 sheet of A5 (8¼x6in/21x15cm) paper

1 Fold the paper in half widthwise and open out then turn the corners along one side in so that they meet on the central crease.

2 Next turn the tip back so that it sits on the far edge of the paper.

3 Fold the tip back so that the new crease lies halfway between the new edge and the original flaps.

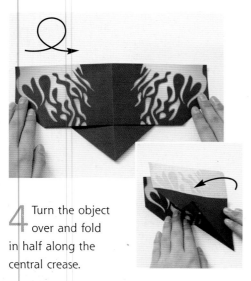

4 Turn the object over and fold in half along the central crease.

5 Place a ruler against the object to make a crisp, angled fold for the wing, starting at the end tip of the plane. Turn over and repeat on the other side to finish.

17 JUMBO JET

The jumbo jet is one of the largest passenger planes and seeing it immediately brings to mind dreams of flying away to distant lands and wonderful vacations. This plane is made from a paper with designs of the jet repeated in every direction—when it is complete let your imagination take you off to exotic beaches or snowy mountains.

Skill rating ● ● ○

You will need
1 sheet of A5 (8¼x6in/21x15cm) paper

PLANES APLENTY

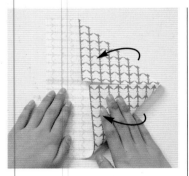

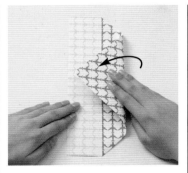

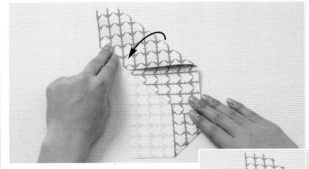

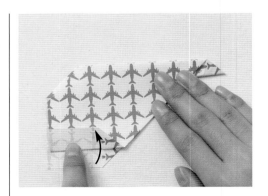

1 Fold the paper in half widthwise and open out then turn the corners along one side in so that they meet on the central crease.

2 Next turn the tip back so that it sits on the far edge of the paper.

3 Fold the far side across at an angle from the center mark so that the front edge lies along the central crease, then repeat on the near side.

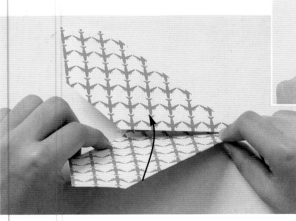

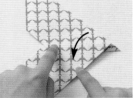

4 Lift up the near half of the object then fold back the wing about ³⁄₈in (1cm) up from the main crease. Turn over and repeat on the other side.

5 Fold back the wing tips to finish.

KITE
crazy

18 JAPANESE CLASSIC KITE

A *yakko*—meaning servant—is traditionally the person drawn on this ancient Japanese *origami* model for children. This cylinder-type kite is not the highest of flyers, but if a group of youngsters run around with kites on short lengths of thread, they will hang in the sky behind them as though the *yakko* are playing tag with each other.

You will need
1 sheet of 6in (15cm) square paper
Scissors
Paper glue
Thread
Stapler
2 12in (30cm) lengths of ribbon

1 Make a crease down the paper through the middle of the design—not the center of the paper—then fold the near side along the edge of the design.

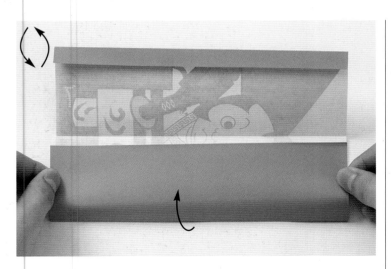

2 Turn the paper round and fold back the other edge, along the outside of the other side of the design.

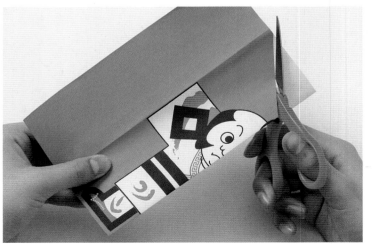

3 Cut out the plain triangle at the top of the design with scissors.

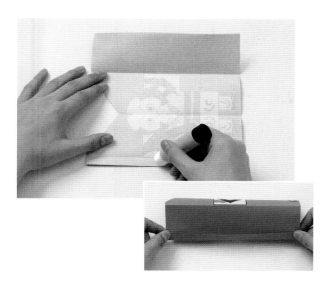

4 Put glue inside the narrow flap then fold forward the wider flap and stick in place.

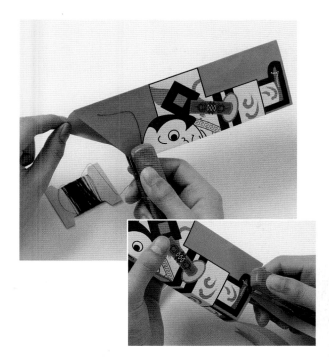

5 Staple a piece of thread to the kite near the top of the design and fix it in place with a granny knot then staple the two ribbons to the base of the kite.

19 HEART KITE

This kite is made in the shape of a romantic heart—perhaps you could fly it as a message to a loved one—with a brilliant sparkling ribbon for the tail. Although this pretty kite is simple to make you will need to take care when cutting the paper with scissors to ensure that you create a nicely rounded heart shape. The heart kite will fly easily on the sweet breeze showing your feelings to the person that matters.

You will need

1 sheet of 6in (15cm) square paper
Scissors
Sticky tape
Thread
Stapler
Drinking straw
12in (30cm) length of sparkling ribbon

1 Fold the paper in half from corner to corner to make a crease, then open it out and cut down the crease approximately 3in (7.5cm).

2 Turn back the two flaps at equal angles and stick them in place with sticky tape. Fold the paper in half then cut out the edge into the shape of half a heart.

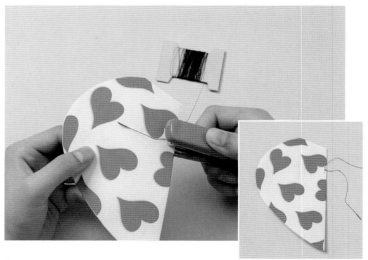

3 Attach a thread to the kite by stapling through both sides of the kite near the top, then fix the thread in place with a knot and cut off any excess.

4 Open out the kite and staple one end of a straw to the widest part. Next staple the other side in place, ensuring the kite is not flat against the straw, then cut off any excess part of the straw.

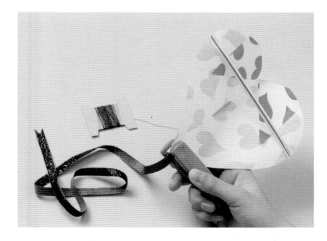

5 Place the end of the ribbon at the bottom rear of the kite and staple in place.

20 CAT KITE

This kite is made from paper with a design of a fun cat on the front; in fact the cat's face is one of the traditional models of Japanese *origami*. Making it is easy but if you want to design your own original cat kite just get some plain paper and draw on the eyes, nose, and mouth yourself—adding the whiskers and eyebrows to give it a bit of character. Make enough and you could end up flying a whole family of cats!

You will need
1 sheet of 6in (15cm) square paper
Thread
Stapler
12in (30cm) length of ribbon

1 Fold the sheet in half from corner to corner and then in half again. Turn over ⅛in (5mm) in from the main crease and make a fold.

2 Open out the sheet and fold forward the two outer points to make the cat's ears.

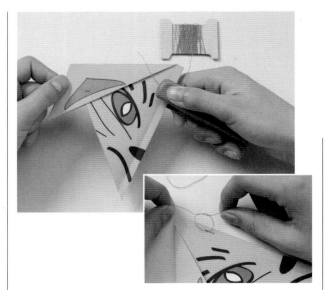

3 Fold in half and attach a thread by stapling through both sides of the kite just inside the central fold, then tie a knot in the thread and cut off any excess.

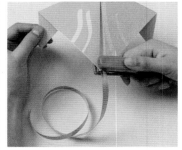

4 Place the end of the ribbon at the bottom of the kite's back and fix with a staple.

21 DOG KITE

The Dog Kite is very similar to the Cat Kite shown on the previous pages, you only need to make one extra fold to give it the appearance of a friendly puppy—which do you prefer? You can make cat and dog kites with your friends and a great game is to see who can fly their kite the highest or keep it in the air for the longest time!

You will need
1 sheet of 6in (15cm) square paper
Thread
Stapler
12in (30cm) length of ribbon

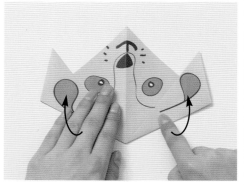

1 Fold the sheet in half from corner to corner and then in half again.

2 Open out the sheet and fold forward the two outer points to make the dog's ears.

3 Turn the paper over and fold back the small triangle at the base.

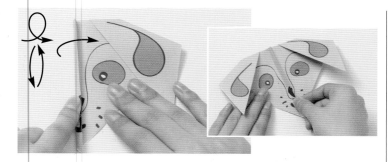

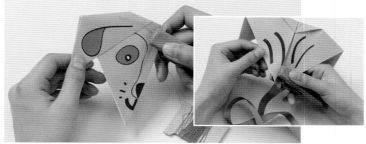

4 Turn the paper back over. Spin the kite through 180° then fold it in half before making a fold 1/8in (5mm) in from the main crease. Open out the paper and pinch the 5mm fold upright.

5 Attach a thread to the kite by stapling through both sides of the kite just inside the central fold, then knot the thread in place. Staple the end of the ribbon to the bottom rear of the kite.

KITE CRAZY

72

22 FLYING SQUIRREL KITE

The flying squirrel glides with the greatest of ease! He leaps from tree to tree while controlling his flight with his long, bushy tail and this kite flies well even on a day with only a light breeze. Ask an adult to help you make the cuts in the drinking straw used to strengthen the sides of the kite because they can be a little tricky to get exactly right. By following the instructions carefully your kite will float in the air for as long as you like.

Skill rating ● ● ●

You will need
2 sheets of 6in (15cm) square paper, one for the kite and one for the tail
Drinking straw
Scissors
Thread
Sticky tape

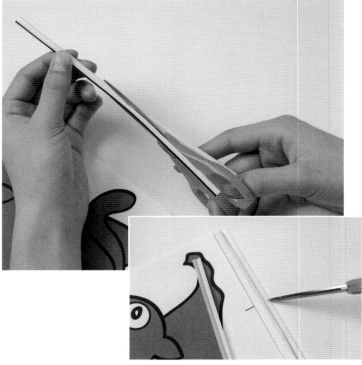

1 Cut a straw in half along its length then place both sides next to the paper and make a small nick to match the mark on the design.

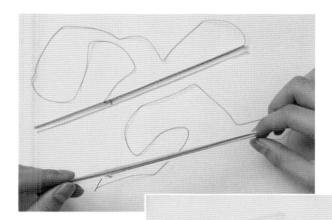

2 Tie the ends of a 18in (45cm) length of thread together and place it in the nick on the straw before pulling it tight and fixing it in place with sticky tape. Repeat.

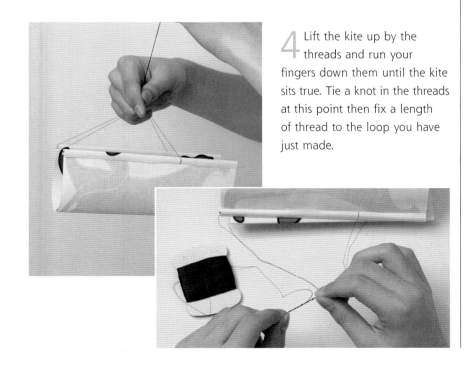

3 Now cut the marks on the side of the design and place the straw on the paper before turning the side over and fixing the straw in place with sticky tape. Repeat on the other side.

4 Lift the kite up by the threads and run your fingers down them until the kite sits true. Tie a knot in the threads at this point then fix a length of thread to the loop you have just made.

5 Cut along the lines of the tail design and fix the longest piece to the rear of the kite in the center.

23 HAWK KITE

As the hawk calmly sweeps across the sky among the clouds he rules over everything he can see. Use strong thread and launch the Hawk Kite onto the wind by running quickly across an open space. When your own kite is high in the air looking down on all the others with its tail streaming out behind it, you, too, will be a king of the sky.

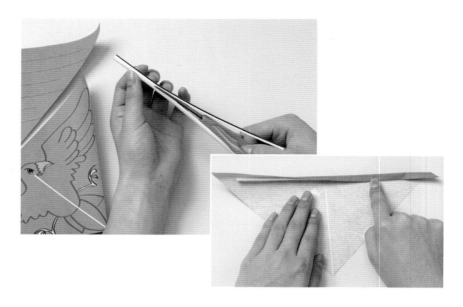

You will need
1 sheet of 6in (15cm) square paper
2 drinking straws
Scissors
Sticky tape
Thread

1 Cut the paper in half to separate the kite from the tail then cut a straw in half along its length. Place one half along the longest side of the paper and fold the paper over, fixing it in place with sticky tape.

2 Cut a ⅛in (5mm) length from the other straw. Knot the end of the thread in place.

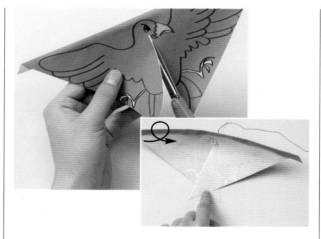

3 Cut up the center line of the design then turn the paper over, place the piece of threaded straw at the end of the cut, and attach it with sticky tape. Fix one half of the paper in place over the other with sticky tape.

4 Cut along the lines of the tail design and fix the longest length to the bottom rear of the kite with tape.

KITE CRAZY

ANIMAL
airforce

24 CICADA

The Japanese summer is very sultry and in the heat the millions of cicadas that live among the trees sound their cries together like an orchestra. The sound of the insect's vigorous calling is one of the most iconic in Japan and has become a symbol of the country's strength as well as the power of nature. This *origami* model is a tribute to the cicada and flies like a boomerang, fluttering through the air and returning to you if you hold it in your fingers and throw it with a good flick of the wrist.

You will need
1 sheet of 6in (15cm) square paper
Scissors

1 Fold the paper in half then open out and fold the other way before cutting it in half with a pair of scissors.

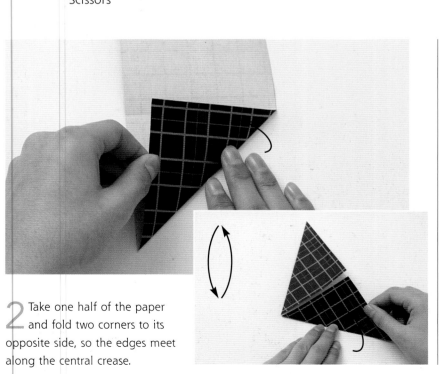

2 Take one half of the paper and fold two corners to its opposite side, so the edges meet along the central crease.

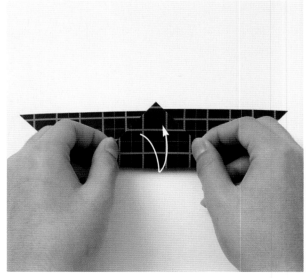

3 Fold the point of the triangle back to the other side of the paper and make a crease.

ANIMAL AIRFORCE

4 Open out and fold up one side of the triangle so that the edge crosses the center point of the long side.

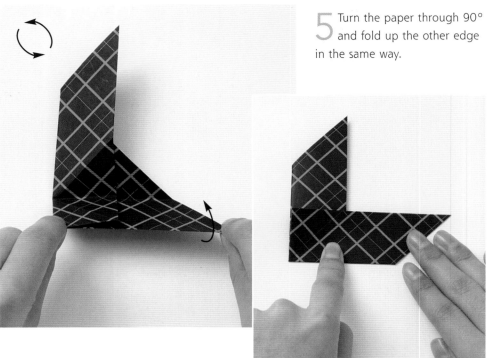

5 Turn the paper through 90° and fold up the other edge in the same way.

6 Lift the bottom fold and open out the diagonal flap at the bottom. Begin to reverse the diagonal creases as you press the horizontal flap back down.

7 When you finish you should be left with a square flap lying flush to the top of the object.

8 Turn in the loose corners of the square so that the edges meet along its center line.

9 Fold the triangle at the bottom of the square across the folds just made and release to make a crease, then use the point of a pencil to open out the pockets on its diagonal edges.

10 Push the flaps made in step 8 into the pockets and flatten so that the design holds in place.

11 Throw the cicada by holding it backward and flicking it forward with a spinning motion.

25 JUMPING FROG

Frogs are renowned for their ability to leap long distances and this model will also jump high in the air when the bottom of its back is lightly pushed with a finger. To make them jump well, the part of the *origami* model that corresponds to frog's back leg must be firmly folded, which can be a little tricky as the paper already has many creases. Try your frog against ones made by your friends and family to see whose leaps the farthest.

Skill rating ● ● ●

You will need
1 sheet of 6in (15cm) square paper

ANIMAL AIRFORCE

1 Fold the paper in half, then open it out and repeat across its other side. Next fold one side in so that its edge lies down the central crease.

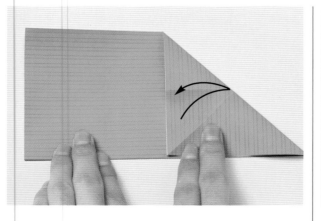

2 Open out the paper and fold one corner across the paper to reach the middle of the opposite side. Open it out and turn over the other corner at the same end.

3 Open out the paper and press in the sides, bringing the end of the paper forward to make a triangle.

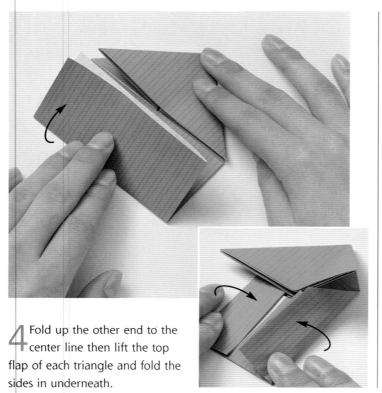

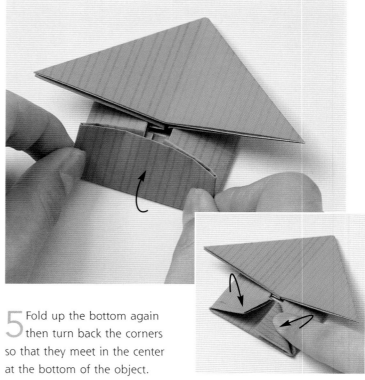

4 Fold up the other end to the center line then lift the top flap of each triangle and fold the sides in underneath.

5 Fold up the bottom again then turn back the corners so that they meet in the center at the bottom of the object.

6 Release the folds, letting the base rise up, then carefully hold the inner flap and pull it out, around, and forward, reversing the crease.

7 Flatten to leave a triangular point at the base then repeat on the other side.

8 Fold the two bottom points across at an angle to create the feet, ensuring the bottom edges are parallel to the base of the object.

9 Turn up the two points of the top triangle so that the outer edges are vertical.

10 Turn up the base, making a fold across the center of the object then turn back the feet halfway down.

11 Make the frog jump by pressing down on the bottom of it's back and releasing.

26 CRANE

The crane is a symbol of peace and a mystical creature in Japan. It is a graceful flyer and this *origami* version is no exception. It's great fun to make a few birds with friends and it always raises a smile when you pull the tail and the wings flap.

Skill rating ● ● ○

You will need
1 sheet of 6in (15cm) square paper

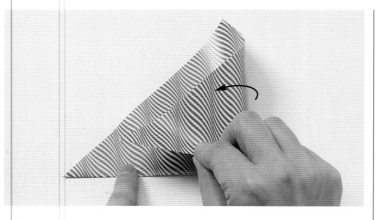

1 Start by folding the paper from corner to corner then fold in half along its longest edge.

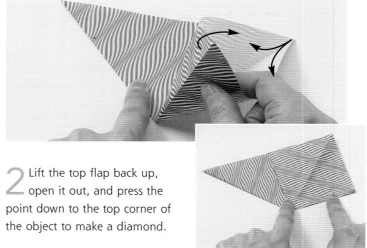

2 Lift the top flap back up, open it out, and press the point down to the top corner of the object to make a diamond.

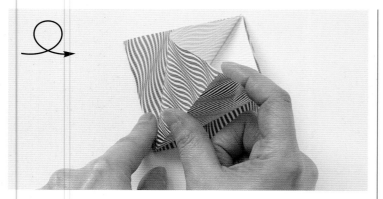

3 Turn the paper over so that the long point is to the right. Lift the point, open out the flap, and press down so the whole object is a diamond.

4 Turn the object clockwise so that the point which cannot be opened out is to the left, then fold the bottom flap up and press down along the center crease. Repeat with the top flap.

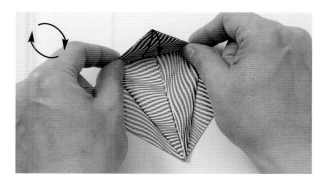

5 Turn the object clockwise again then make a crease by folding down the top point across the edges of the two folds made in the previous step.

6 Open out the folds from the previous two steps. Lift the top flap backward, so that the two sides meet along the center, creating a long diamond shape.

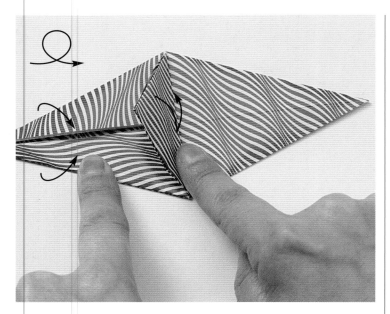

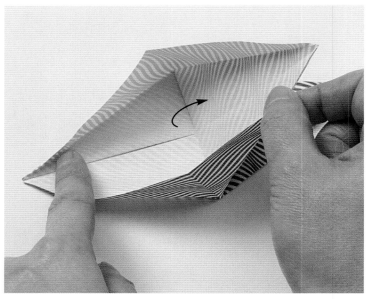

7 Turn the paper over and fold the sides into the center then turn back the central triangle to make a crease.

8 Again, open out the folds and lift the top flap to the right to bring the two sides together in the center.

ANIMAL AIRFORCE

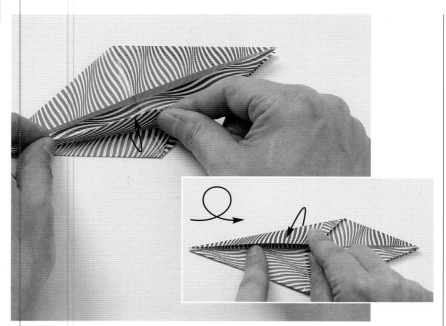

9 Turn back the nearest flap so that the edge runs up the center line then turn the object over and fold back the flap on the same side.

10 Turn both ends of the object up at an angle so that they sit opposite each other.

11 Holding the wider leg of the object, release the narrower one and open it out. Now reverse the central crease and press both sides of the body together to make the bird's neck.

12 Repeat the last step on the wider leg to create the tail, ensuring that it ends up sitting at an angle inside the main body of the object.

CRANE

13 Turn down the end of the neck to make the head, then open it and reverse the fold so that it sits at an angle.

14 Turn down the wings of the bird as close to the body as possible.

15 Make the wings flap by pulling up on the tail and releasing.

27 BALLOON RABBIT

The balloon is a popular model in Japan and this rabbit version is a fun alternative take on the original design. It makes use of special folds that show flashes of the paper's colored side against the white background, which you can decorate with a rabbit's eyes, whiskers, and a fluffy tail. Once you've done this it's ready to fly, just bounce the balloon in the palm of your hand.

You will need
1 sheet of 6in (15cm) square paper

1 Fold the paper in half, then again across its width. With the horizontal fold at the top, lift the top flap, open it out, and refold it in a triangle.

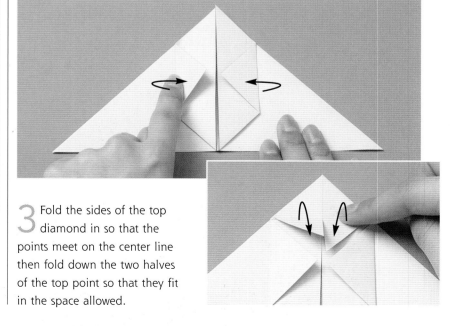

2 Turn over the paper and repeat, then turn the top flaps of the two outer corners up to the center point so that the edges meet along the middle.

3 Fold the sides of the top diamond in so that the points meet on the center line then fold down the two halves of the top point so that they fit in the space allowed.

ANIMAL AIRFORCE

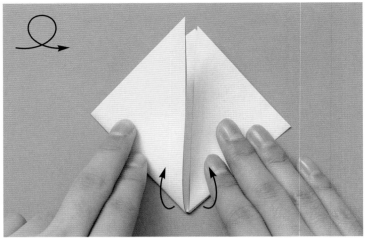

4 Turn the newly folded top points across the edges of the triangles to make creases, then tuck the ends inside the pockets on the same edges.

5 Turn the object over and fold up the two outer corners to the top point to make a diamond.

6 Turn the right-hand point round the side of the rear flap to make a crease then bring it to the front again and fold it in between the front and rear flaps. Repeat on the left-hand side.

7 Fold over the top flaps at an angle so that the edges just cover the top of the vertical side.

8 Gently open out the flap by pressing down on the tip. Repeat on the second flap.

9 Now slowly push back the top on both sides to make a horizontal fold between the two widest points of the flap.

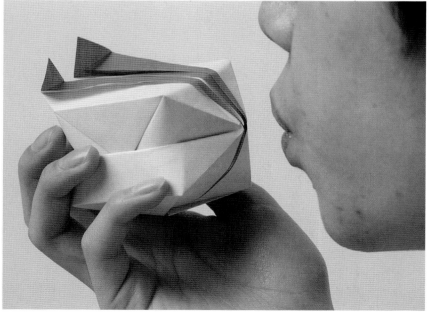

10 Turn the object over and fold in the top and bottom triangles to make horizontal creases.

11 Gently blow into the hole at the bottom of the object, inflating the paper into a balloon, teasing open the folds with your fingers as you do so.

28 RED DRAGONFLY

The brightly colored dragonfly dances through the air, whizzing back and forth among tall grasses and over water. This model is similar to the crane on page 88 until the point when the wings are split with a cut from a pair of scissors. Once you have mastered the technique you can make a selection of dragonflies in different colors and hang them in a room to remind you of those fun days of summer.

You will need
1 sheet of 6in (15cm) square paper
Scissors

1 Start by folding the paper from corner to corner then again along its longest edge.

2 Lift the top flap back up, open it out, and press the point down to the top of the object to make a diamond. Turn the whole thing over and repeat.

3 Turn the object clockwise so that the point which cannot be opened out is to the left, then fold the bottom flap up and press down along the central crease. Repeat with the top flap. Fold the left point across the edges of the two folds just made to make a crease.

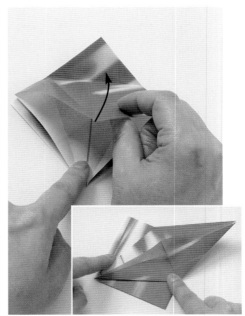

4 Lift the top flap and turn it backward, bringing the two sides together along the middle, leaving a long diamond shape.

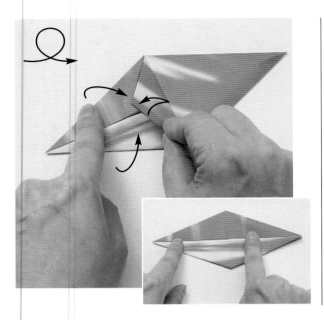

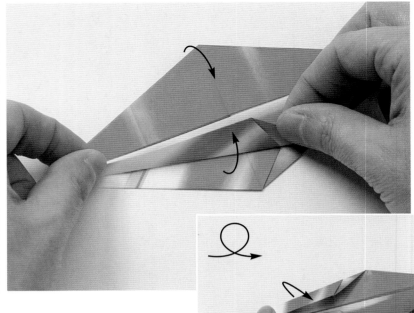

ANIMAL AIRFORCE

5 Turn the paper over and fold the sides into the center then turn back the central triangle over the edges to make a crease. Again, lift the top flap and turn it backward, bring the two sides together, leaving a long diamond shape.

6 Turn back both flaps on the top of the object so that their edges run up the divided center line, then turn the object over and repeat on the reverse.

7 Turn both ends of the object up at an angle so that they sit opposite each other.

8 Holding one leg of the object, release the other and open it out.

9 Now reverse the central crease and press both sides of the body back together around it to make the dragonfly's neck.

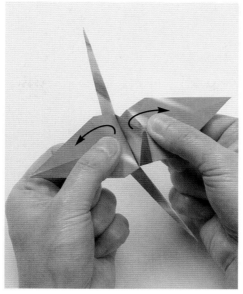

10 Repeat on the other leg to form the dragonfly's tail.

11 Turn down the wings of the dragonfly, making the folds as near the body as possible.

12 Gently pull the wings apart to flatten the protruding triangle of paper, then push it down inside the dragonfly.

13 Carefully cut around the points of the wings to round them off, then cut up their centers to split them in half.

14 Turn over the end of the neck and then reverse the central fold and press the end flat to make the head.

29 BUTTERFLY

This tumbling Butterfly with its beautiful dappled wings resembles this most colorful of insects. It isn't launched with a throw like an airplane; instead it is dropped from as high as possible and as it falls it spins round and round on itself while also rotating—just as though the butterfly is fluttering across a garden from one flower to the next.

You will need
1 sheet of 6in (15cm) square paper

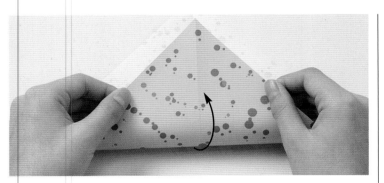

1 Fold the paper in half from corner to corner to make a crease then open it out and fold the other corners together.

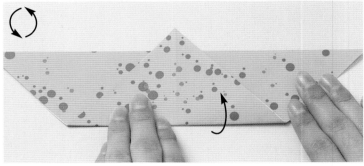

2 Spin the object abround and fold the tip over so that the end projects about 3/8in (1cm) over the paper's edge.

3 Spin the object through 90° and then fold it in half along the central crease.

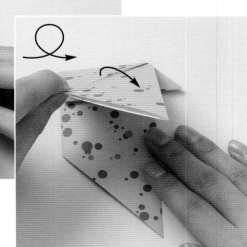

4 Fold down the wing and turn the paper over and fold down the other side to match.

TOYS
for takeoff

30 ANGEL BOX

The Angel Box is a new take on the traditional *origami* balloon, giving it the wings it needs to rise up into the heavens. The classic designs have been perfected over many centuries so new versions ensure the old ideas remain fresh. Place the Angel Box on the palm and bounce it high. It will rise like a ball but its wings seem to give it a little extra boost, allowing it to sit in the air for just a little bit longer.

You will need
1 sheet of 6in (15cm) square paper

1 Fold the paper in half twice then lift the top half and refold it into a triangle. Repeat on the other side.

2 Fold the two outer corners to meet at the top point then turn the paper over and repeat on the other side.

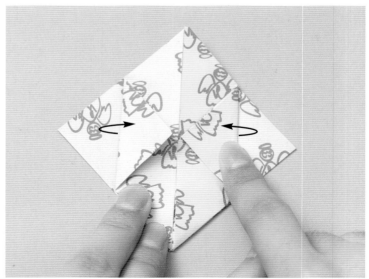

3 Fold in the outer points of the top layer so that they meet on the center line.

TOYS FOR TAKEOFF

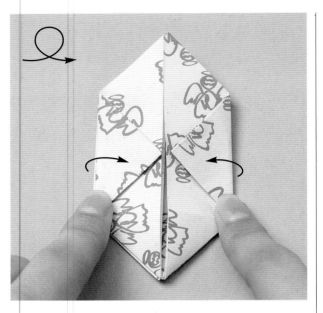

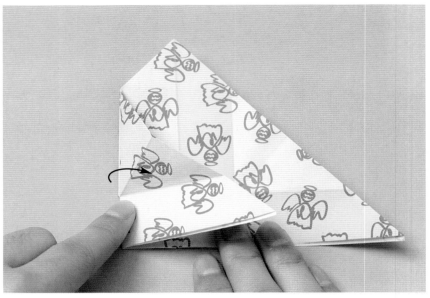

4 Turn the paper over and repeat on the other side.

5 Open out the top layer of the object into a triangle, then fold over the left-hand point along the crease to the left of the center fold line.

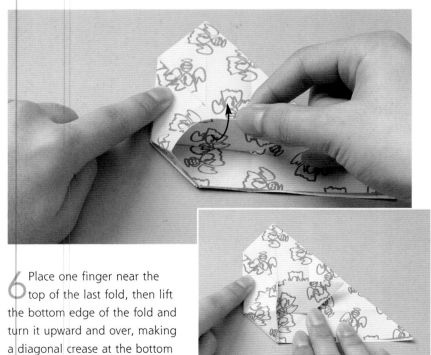

6 Place one finger near the top of the last fold, then lift the bottom edge of the fold and turn it upward and over, making a diagonal crease at the bottom left of the object.

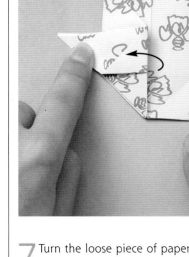

7 Turn the loose piece of paper over the vertical edge so that it sticks out to the left.

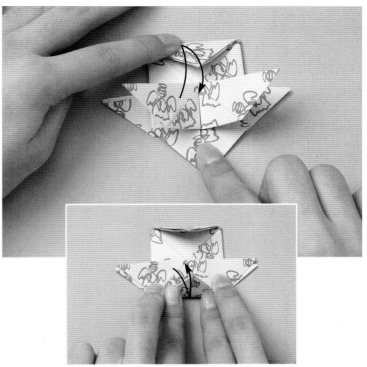

8 Repeat on the right-hand side of the top layer then turn the whole paper open and repeat steps 5 through 7.

9 Make a crease by folding the top triangle forward over the horizontal edge. Release and repeat with the bottom triangle.

10 Gently open out the creases and hold the object with the hole in the bottom nearest you.

11 Carefully inflate the Angel Box by blowing through the hole, helping to form the shape with your fingers.

31 HELICOPTER

The Helicopter is a very satisfying model to make as it is extremely easy to fold, and when dropped from a height, it rotates round and round just like a helicopter, spinning evenly as floats toward the ground. Remember to take care with the creases so that the sides of the model match exactly—if the model is lopsided and needs a little extra weight on one side to make the rotation even, just add a paper clip where necessary.

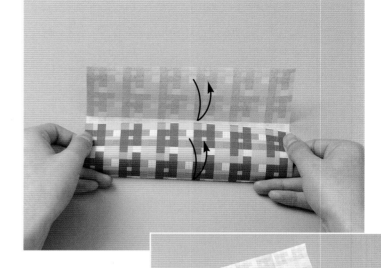

You will need
1 sheet of 6in (15cm) square paper
Scissors

1 Fold the sheet into three equal widths then use the scissors to cut along one of the creases, keeping the narrow piece of paper.

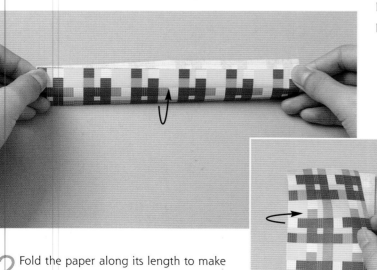

2 Fold the paper along its length to make a crease then open it out and make a second crease by folding it in half across its width.

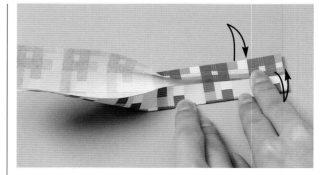

3 Fold both sides into the center, making creases from one end to the center point marked by the crease made in the previous step.

108

TOYS FOR TAKEOFF

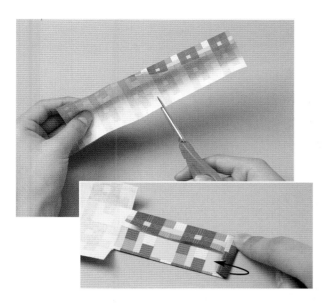

4 Cut along the same crease on both sides to the creases made in the previous step and fold the edges flat. Turn over the end twice to keep the folds in place.

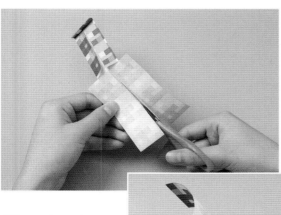

5 Cut down the central crease from the other end to the center then turn the ends over your finger in opposing directions to make the helicopter's rotors.

32 MAGIC RING

On first glance you wouldn't think this paper ring was a good flyer, but the magic of this project ring is that it flies extraordinarily well. The trick is to get much of the paper's weight into the narrow band that forms the cental axis. This gives the ring natural rotation, which allows every throw to be straight. You will need to master the knack but once you do your friends will be amazed by this fantastic flyer.

You will need
1 sheet of A5 (8¼x6in/21x15cm) paper

1 Find the center point by folding the paper in half twice then opening out.

TOYS FOR TAKEOFF

2 Fold the paper diagonally through the center point so that the creases end up directly on top of one another to ensure that the sides are parallel.

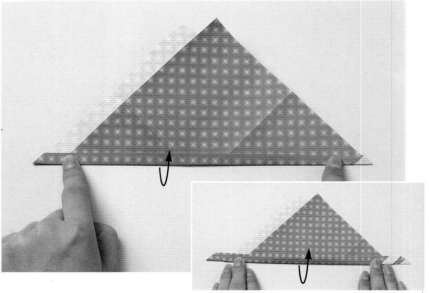

3 Now turn the bottom edge up, using the outer points of the object as the crease points before rolling the bottom up again, halving the width of the flap just made. Next turn over the bottom flap once more.

4 Join the ring together by tucking the left-hand side into the back of the right-hand side and finish by tucking the loose end into the front.

5 Throw the ring by holding it from underneath with your middle finger and flicking it forward.

33 NINJA KNIFE

A *ninja* was a professional spy in feudal Japan who had been highly trained in stealth and secrecy. The gleaming blades of his favorite weapon, the throwing-knife, are replicated in this traditional paper model. Even when made in *origami* it flies with power so be extra careful not to throw it near your friends as its sharp points could harm their eyes.

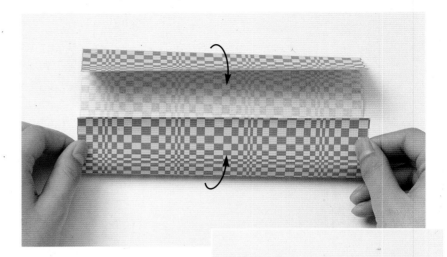

You will need
2 sheets of 6in (15cm) square paper

1 Fold the first sheet of paper in half to make a crease then open it out and fold both edges in to meet in the middle. Fold the paper in half again along the central crease.

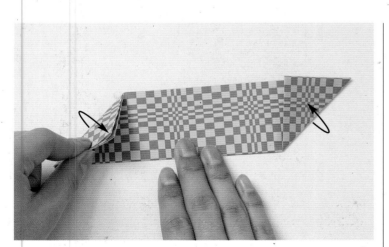
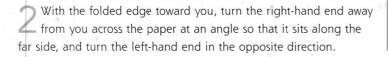

2 With the folded edge toward you, turn the right-hand end away from you across the paper at an angle so that it sits along the far side, and turn the left-hand end in the opposite direction.

3 Take the second sheet and repeat the first two steps but this time turn the right-hand end toward you and the left-hand end away from you.

TOYS FOR TAKEOFF

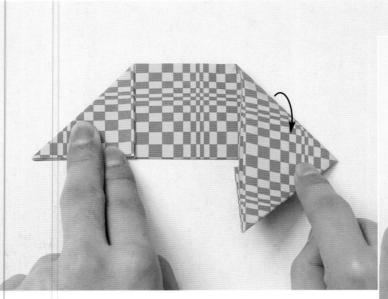

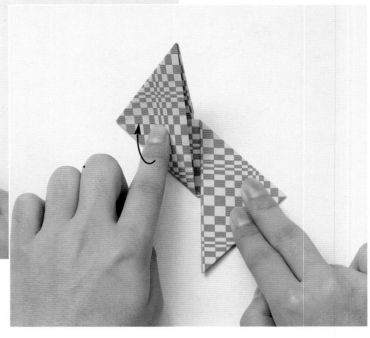

4 Turn the right-hand end of the first sheet forward at an angle so that the top edge now runs vertically down across the paper, then repeat on the left-hand side turning the end away from you.

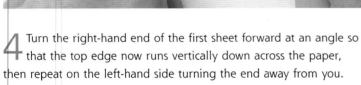

5 Repeat on the second sheet, this time turning the right-hand end away from you and bringing the left-hand end toward you.

6 Turn over the first sheet and place it as shown, then spin the second sheet through 90° and place it on top of the first sheet.

7 Fold the two tips of the bottom sheet over so that they tuck into the flaps of the top sheet.

8 Turn the whole object over and tuck the bottom tip of the second sheet into the flap on the top of the first sheet.

9 Finish by carefully tucking the final tip into the remaining flap and gently pressing the object into shape.

34 APOLLO ROCKET

The Apollo rocket took astronauts to the Moon, taking men farther from Earth than ever before. This *origami* model is made with paper that is a reminder of adventures through space. Although the rocket will not fly, it can sit on a child's bedside table or be hung on a thread from the ceiling. Perhaps you could fold a series of rockets and pretend they are embarking on intergalactic missions above your head.

You will need
1 sheet of 6in (15cm) square paper

1 Fold the sheet in half to make a crease from corner to corner then open it and fold in the other direction.

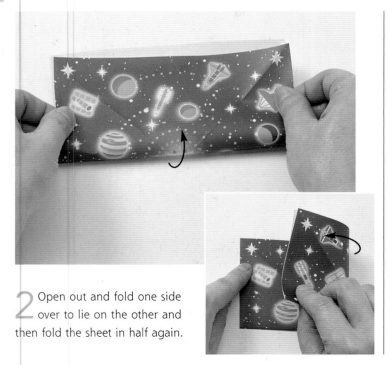

2 Open out and fold one side over to lie on the other and then fold the sheet in half again.

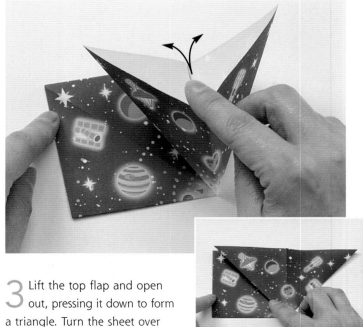

3 Lift the top flap and open out, pressing it down to form a triangle. Turn the sheet over and repeat on the other side.

TOYS FOR TAKEOFF

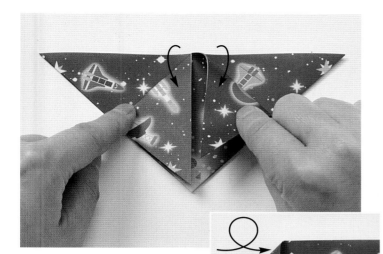

4 Fold forward the two outer points of the top flap so that they meet at the bottom of the object. Turn the object over and repeat so that you are left with a diamond shape.

5 Spin the object so that the loose points face away from you, then lift the left-hand flap, open it out, and refold into a square. Repeat on the right-hand side.

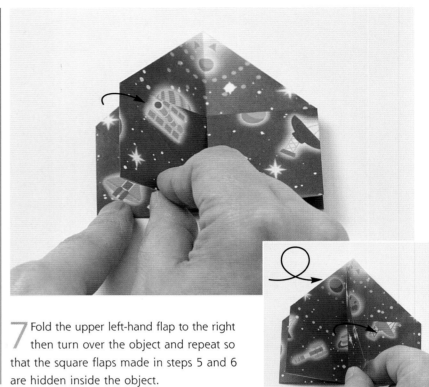

6 Turn the paper over and repeat on the other side.

7 Fold the upper left-hand flap to the right then turn over the object and repeat so that the square flaps made in steps 5 and 6 are hidden inside the object.

8 Fold in both sides so that the edges meet along the central crease then turn the paper over and repeat.

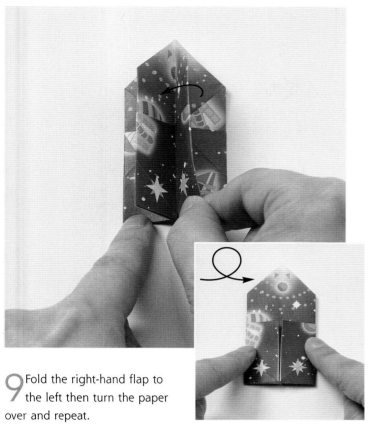

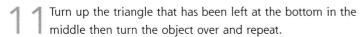

9 Fold the right-hand flap to the left then turn the paper over and repeat.

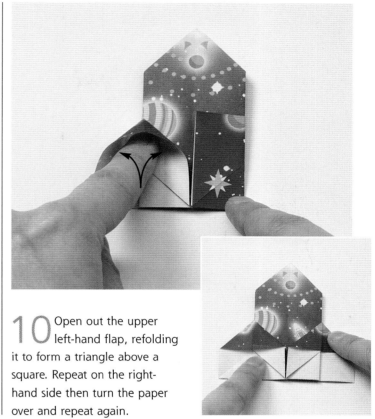

10 Open out the upper left-hand flap, refolding it to form a triangle above a square. Repeat on the right-hand side then turn the paper over and repeat again.

11 Turn up the triangle that has been left at the bottom in the middle then turn the object over and repeat.

12 To finish gently open out the four supports of the rocket so that they are evenly spaced.

35 CHALLENGER ROCKET

The final model is as close as *origami* gets to a real rocket—though this does mean it is quite challenging to make. When you have finished folding it, carefully inflate it like the *origami* balloon and then place it on the end of a drinking straw so that it can be launched with one quick breath—can yours replicate the power of the largest rockets and reach the Moon?

You will need
1 sheet of 6in (15cm) square paper

1 Fold the sheet in half from corner to corner then fold in half again.

TOYS FOR TAKEOFF

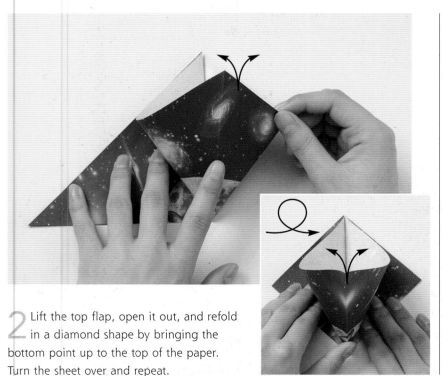

2 Lift the top flap, open it out, and refold in a diamond shape by bringing the bottom point up to the top of the paper. Turn the sheet over and repeat.

3 Fold the left-hand flap into the center so that the outer edge runs up the middle.

4 Lift up the flap and open it out, refolding it so that it is centered on the paper.

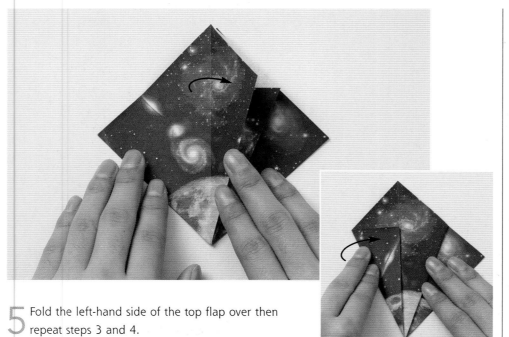

5 Fold the left-hand side of the top flap over then repeat steps 3 and 4.

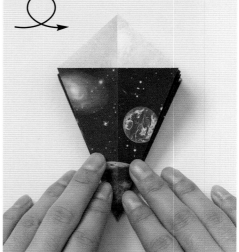

6 Next turn the whole object over and repeat folding in the left-hand flap until you have done it four times in all.

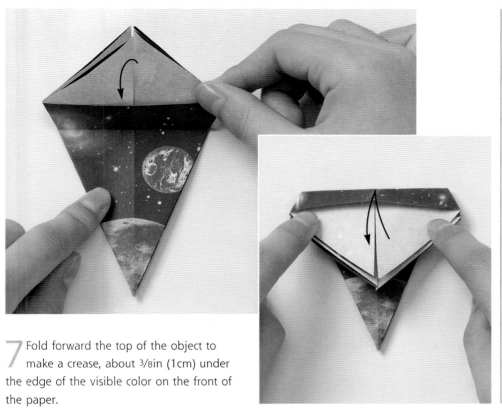

7 Fold forward the top of the object to make a crease, about 3/8in (1cm) under the edge of the visible color on the front of the paper.

8 Turn the top flap on the right-hand side over to the left.

123

9 Fold forward the upper flap along the crease made in step 7 and flatten the two central pieces that are sticking up.

CHALLENGER ROCKET

10 Turn the object over, fold the right-hand flap to the left before once again folding the top forward and flattening.

11 Again turn the right-hand flap to the left and fold forward the top flap.

12 Fold over three flaps so that the last remaining tall flap is uppermost then turn down the top point in the same way.

13 Reform the object so that there are two flaps on each side, then fold in
the sides of each flap to make winglets.

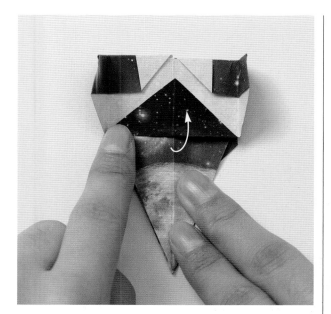

14 Turn over the loose triangle of paper inside
each flap so that it is flush with the winglets.

15 Gently open out the flaps and, holding them apart in your fingers,
carefully blow into the hole at the base of the object to give it shape.

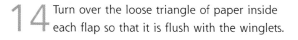

USEFUL INFORMATION

SUPPLIERS Origami paper is available at most good paper stores or online. Amazon and eBay are good sources for paper, or try typing "origami paper" into an internet search engine to find a whole range of stores, selling a wide variety of paper, who will send packages directly to your home address.

USA

A.C. MOORE
www.acmoore.com
Stores nationwide
TEL: 1-888-ACMOORE (1-888-226-6673)

CRAFTS, ETC.
www.craftsetc.com
Online store
TEL: 1-800-888-0321

HOBBY LOBBY
www.hobbylobby.com
Stores nationwide

JO-ANN FABRIC AND CRAFT STORE
www.joann.com
Stores nationwide
TEL: 1-888-739-4120

MICHAELS STORES
www.michaels.com
Stores nationwide
TEL: 1-800-MICHAELS (1-800-642-4235)

HAKUBUNDO
www.hakubundo.com
1600 Kapiolani Blvd. Suite 121, Honolulu, Hawaii 96814
TEL: (808) 947-5503
FAX: (808) 947-5602
E-mail:hakubundo@hakubundo.com

UK

HOBBYCRAFT
www.hobbycraft.co.uk
TEL: +44 (0) 1202 596100

JP-BOOKS
www.jpbooks.co.uk/en
c/o Mitsukoshi, Dorland House
14-20 Regent Street, London SW1Y 4PH
Open: Mon-Sat 10:00-18:30, Sun 10:30-16:30
TEL: +44 (0)20 7839 4839
FAX: +44 (0)20 7925 0346
E-mail: info@jpbooks.co.uk

JAPAN CENTRE
www.japancentre.com
14-20 Regent St, London SW1Y 4PH
Open: Mon-Sat 10:00-21:00, Sun 11:00-19:00
TEL: +44 (0) 20 3405 1150
FAX: +44 (0) 20 7930 7754
E-mail: enquiry@japancentre.com

THE JAPANESE SHOP (online only)
www.thejapaneseshop.co.uk
TEL: +44 (0)1423 545020
FAX: +44 (0)1423 540191
E-mail: info@thejapaneseshop.co.uk

FRANCE

CULTURE JAPON S.A.S.
Store in Maison du la culture du Japon
101 bis quai Branly 75015, Paris
TEL: +33 (1) 45 79 02 00
FAX: +33 (1) 45 79 02 09
E-mail: culturejpt@wanadoo.fr

BOOKS

The Simple Art of Japanese Papercrafts, Mari Ono (CICO Books)
Origami for Children, Mari Ono and Roshin Ono (CICO Books)

WEBSITES

Origami Club:
en.origami-club.com

OrigamiUSA:
www.origami-usa.org

British Origami Society:
www.britishorigami.info

INDEX

From left to right: Geoff Dann, Marcus Harvey, Takumasa Ono, Robin Gurdon, Roshin Ono.
Photo taken by Mari Ono

ACKNOWLEDGMENTS

I've been extremely fortunate that a great many people have helped with the creation of this book—to all of them I say a very big thank you. My editor, Robin Gurdon, has helped me throughout with skill and knowledge and I'm also immensely grateful to the photographer, Geoff Dann, and his assistant, Marcus Harvey.

Friends and family have been tremendously supportive, in particular Takumasa, my husband, who designed some of the paper plane models as well as many of the wonderful origami papers used in this book, and our son, Roshin, who acted as the model for all the projects, and also designed some paper plane models. I cannot thank both of them enough for their encouragement.

I would also like to say many thanks to Cindy Richards, Sally Powell, Paul Tilby, and Pete Jorgensen of CICO Books as well as Trina Dalziel, who styled and designed the background of all the projects in this book. Her wonderful sensibility has made this a very happy book— I wish to express my gratitude to her.